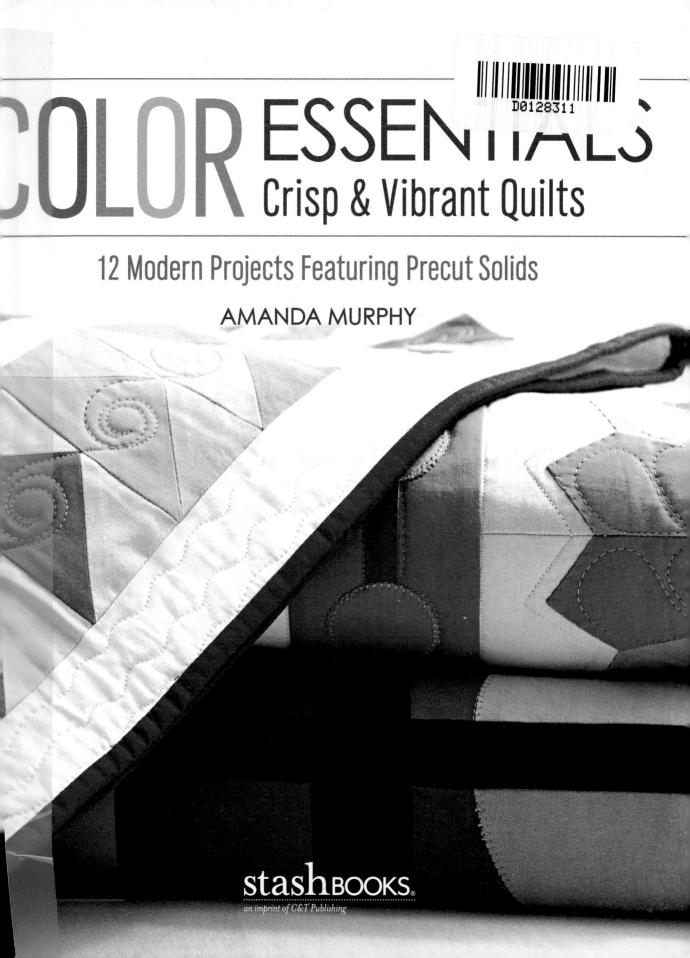

COLOR ESSENTIALS
Crisp & Vibrant Quilts

12 Modern Projects Featuring Precut Solids

AMANDA MURPHY

stashBOOKS®

an imprint of C&T Publishing

PUBLISHER: Amy Marson

CREATIVE DIRECTOR: Gailen Runge

ART DIRECTOR / COVER DESIGNER: Kristy Zacharias

EDITOR: Deb Rowden

TECHNICAL EDITORS: Alison M. Schmidt and Susan Hendrickson

BOOK DESIGNER: April Mostek

PRODUCTION COORDINATORS: Jessica Jenkins and Jenny Davis

PRODUCTION EDITOR: Joanna Burgarino

ILLUSTRATORS: Amanda Murphy and Jessica Jenkins

PHOTO ASSISTANT: Mary Peyton Peppo

PHOTOGRAPHY by Diane Pedersen and Nissa Brehmer of C&T Publishing, Inc., unless otherwise noted

Published by Stash Books, an imprint of C&T Publishing, Inc., P.O. Box 1456, Lafayette, CA 94549

Library of Congress Cataloging-in-Publication Data

Murphy, Amanda, 1971-

Color essentials : crisp & vibrant quilts : 12 modern projects featuring precut solids / Amanda Murphy.

  pages cm

ISBN 978-1-60705-709-3 (soft cover)

1. Patchwork--Patterns. 2. Quilting--Patterns. 3. Color in the textile industries.

TT835.M8455 2013

746.46--dc23

2013011483

Contents

I would like to thank...

the countless generations of quilters who have made the world a more beautiful place.

Acknowledgments

"I'm not creative." I've heard that from quilters countless times in classes I have both taught and taken. It simply isn't true. Quilters are some of the most creative people I have ever met. What's more, many quilters have an instinctual feel for how to work with color that they have learned from working with fabric—often without even realizing it.

Color Essentials—Crisp & Vibrant Quilts is about releasing the joy of the creative process to produce a handcrafted, truly unique work of art—possibly something you might have imagined as being beyond your ability to create. If you are a beginning quilter, *Color Essentials—Crisp & Vibrant Quilts* will help you learn the basic principles of working with combinations of different hues. If you are an intermediate or advanced quilter, it will help push you beyond your comfort zone and add new color knowledge to your "design toolbox."

Color Essentials—Crisp & Vibrant Quilts comes fast on the heels of my first book, *Modern Holiday*, and again I'd like to thank Amy Marson, my editors Deb Rowden and Alison Schmidt, my designer April Mostek, and the wonderful staff at C&T Publishing for being so supportive of this book and the modern quilting community in general. Robert Kaufman was my other special partner in this project. The company's wide range of solids and commitment to providing charm packs, roll-ups, and fat quarter bundles in varied hues make producing these projects in an infinite number of uniquely different color palettes both convenient and affordable. In fact, the Kona Sunrise and Sunset palettes were created specifically for this book. Both quilt shops and individuals will appreciate the fact that the projects can be produced with precuts plus a little added yardage for sashing, borders, and binding.

Most projects are sewn in either the Sunrise, Sunset, or Bright palette, and in many projects I show examples of multiple palettes. The Pastel palette is also an option. For large projects, digital mock-ups of four alternative palettes are also shown, to give you an idea of other color possibilities.

As with the projects in *Modern Holiday*, all the projects presented in this book were sewn on a Bernina 580e, a wonderful sewing and embroidery machine with the unsurpassed stitch quality for which Bernina is known. Special thanks to Bernina of America and to Drusilla Munnell and the staff of Sew Much Fun, my local Bernina dealer and quilt shop in Lowell, North Carolina, who have provided enthusiastic support for all my creative endeavors in this industry.

Aurifil, Sulky, the Warm Company, and Clover Needlecraft all provided their great products for these projects. You can find specifics about what I used in the project instructions and can reference company information in the Supplies/Source List section (page 143).

Finally, I'd like to thank Deborah Norris of Deborah's Quilting in Gastonia, North Carolina. Her free-form longarm work adds a special touch to projects, and you can see the details of that work especially well on these quilts made from solids. I find her quilting inspirational and I hope you do too.

So let's get started experimenting with design and color through fabric ...

A RAINBOW of Possibilities

Unlock the mysteries of color with fabric!

Color, Color, Glorious Color!

For many quilters, there is nothing more exciting than a pile of brightly colored fabrics. There are so many hues and an almost infinite number of ways to combine them! Freeing yourself of any preconceived notions about color allows you to discover different combinations and really push the creative envelope. Yet the unlimited possibilities can also be intimidating at times. This book seeks to address these issues.

As much as I love prints, I have always admired the graphic quality of antique quilts comprised of solids. The Amish were particularly adept at producing quilts with simple yet dynamic graphic qualities. Experimenting with solids results in a deep understanding of how color functions. It is my hope that you will be inspired to experiment with some of these projects and apply the knowledge and confidence you gain to future projects.

We are so lucky to have the wide variety of fabrics that are available today. In fact, it is the beautiful range of hues available that inspired *Color Essentials—Crisp & Vibrant Quilts*. I have worked closely with Robert Kaufman Fabrics to develop precut packages of fabric that allow you to experiment with color and produce projects that are affordable, individual, and beautiful.

Let's Get Started...

Most quilters are familiar with the color wheel and its three primary colors of red, yellow, and blue, with the secondary colors of green, violet, and orange nestled in between. Tertiary colors comprise primary colors mixed with secondary colors. All the pure colors featured on a color wheel are referred to as hues. Adding white to a hue produces a tint; adding black produces a shade.

Colors directly across the color wheel from each other are referred to as complementary. (Interestingly, the darker colors we see in nature are usually reproduced by adding a touch of a complementary color to a specific hue, rather than by adding black.) Complementary colors can produce very lively and dynamic designs. Colors next to each other on the color wheel are referred to as analogous. Analogous palettes can be quite beautiful and restful.

This color wheel is unique—it shows how the available Kona palettes fit into the range of possible colors. Look for more information on Kona palettes on pages 20-27.

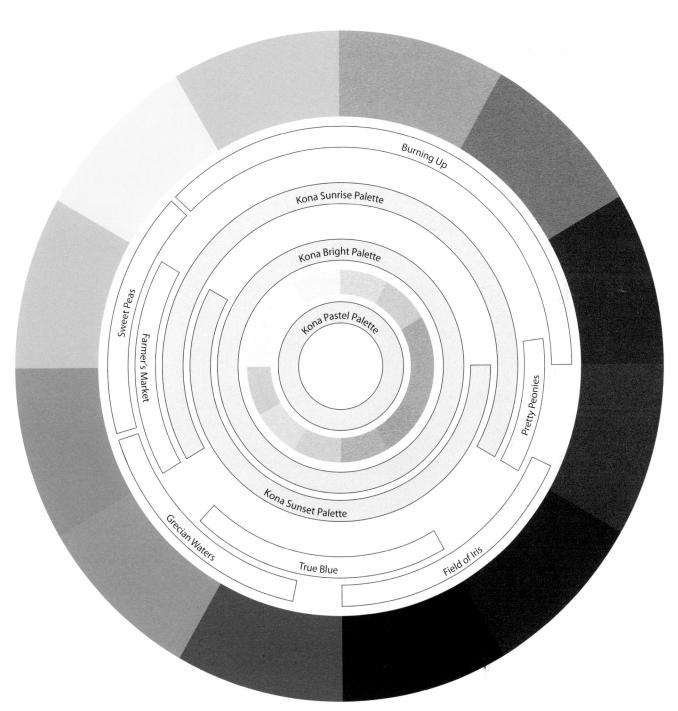

The color wheel and its Kona equivalents

Color Schemes

One way to start thinking about the possibilities of a quilt's design is to consider a color palette that you might like to work with. Perhaps you would like to work with a warm palette of yellows, oranges, and maybe even a touch of pink or green?

Warm palettes

Or perhaps a cool palette might be more to your taste, with soft blues and cool purples?

Note how pink and green tones can work with either a cool or warm palette. Colors aren't always strictly warm or cool; it is how they work in combination with other colors that defines them.

By choosing a light background that matches the general color scheme, you can create a soft look, as in *City Lights* (page 57) or *Iridescence* (page 89). Electing to use a hue on the opposite side of the color wheel from the general color scheme will produce a dynamic look, as evidenced by *Spring Blooms* (page 121).

Cool palettes

You can also choose to use hues that are adjacent on the color wheel to produce a soft look with an analogous color scheme.

Analogous palettes

Adding in a hue from the opposite side of the color wheel from the general color scheme adds movement and interest. I usually refer to this as a "poison" hue because it doesn't fit into the general color scheme, but adding it into the mix can yield dynamic results. It can bring a great deal more visual interest to the quilt, and used sparingly in areas where extra impact is needed, it can draw the viewer's eye from one element to another.

Example of color palettes with corresponding "poison" hues

Swatches displaying analogous color schemes with "poison" accents

Kona Palettes

Kona precuts make playing with color easy and affordable! Pairing them with different background colors allows you to experiment with an infinite variety of color combinations.

The majority of projects in this book are made from roll-ups (2½″ × width of fabric strips), charm packs (5″ × 5″ squares), or fat quarter bundles (18″ × 20″ pieces), juxtaposed against a variety of background fabrics.

Kona precuts come in the Sunrise palette, which covers the warmer side of the color wheel; the Sunset palette, which covers the cooler side of the color wheel; and the Bright palette, which includes selections from the entire color wheel. The Pastel palette also includes selections from the entire color wheel, but they have been lightened considerably. All of the projects in this book are made using the first three palettes. The wonderful thing about these palettes is that you can be assured that the colors in them will work beautifully together. Completely new looks can be achieved by varying the sashing, background, and borders. Whether you choose Kona Sunrise, Sunset, Bright, or Pastel precuts, you are sure to create a unique project and learn a lot about color along the way. Have fun!

The Sunrise and Sunset palettes are both available as charm packs and 2½″ roll-ups with 42 colors each. Smaller selections of the Sunrise and Sunset palettes, comprising 23 colors each, are available as fat quarter bundles. You can see the Sunrise palette at work in *City Lights* (page 57) and *On Pointe* (page 95). Note how the Sunset palette is softened when placed on a darker cool background in *City Lights*, whereas the hue variety is heightened on the more contrasting light blue background in *On Pointe*.

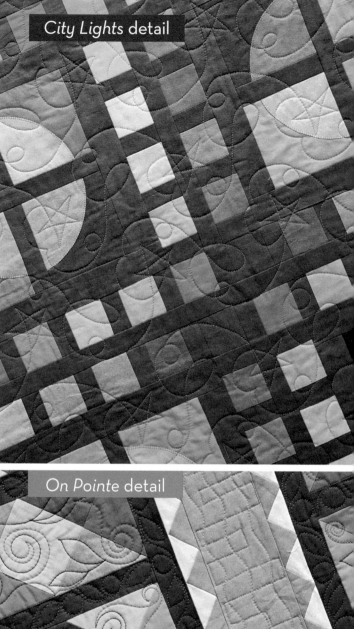

City Lights detail

On Pointe detail

The Sunrise palette's warm hues contrast dynamically with the crisp, white background of *Circus* (page 129), and the yo-yos enhance the playful look. Those same colors are softened when placed on a background that is also warm, as is evident in *Iridescence* (page 89) and *Confetti* (page 113). Note how different the effect is when that same palette is contrasted with cool aqua hues in *Spring Blooms* (page 121)!

Circus detail

Confetti detail

Spring Blooms detail

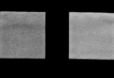

The Bright palette and the Pastel palette both come in charm packs and roll-ups. The Bright palette is particularly effective on a black or white background, as featured in the *City Lights* (page 57) and *Stairways* (page 69) quilts, respectively. A selection of colors in the Bright palette is also used in the irregularly shaped *Color Burst* (page 103).

Color Burst detail

Additional Kona fat quarter bundles are available in specific hues, with delectable names like Fields of Iris and Grecian Waters. These fat quarter bundles can be used in combination with each other to produce beautiful analogous quilts like *Lollipop* (page 79). Or try combining complementary hues, like True Blue and Burning Up, for a completely different look.

The following pages display the exact composition of the Sunrise, Sunset, Bright, and Pastel palettes. To make things easy, I've included background colors that work successfully with each set of precuts, but don't be afraid to experiment and try out new combinations. By no means should you feel limited to these fabric combinations; there are a myriad of possibilities to create beautiful projects.

Kona Sunrise Palette

The Kona Sunrise palette is available in charm packs and 2½" × WOF strips in roll-ups of 42 colors. A selection of 23 of these colors (indicated by asterisks) comes in fat quarter bundles.

Suggested Backgrounds

K001-1387
White

K001-1216
Maize

K001-21
Honey Dew

K001-1275
Pale Mint

K001-1176
Ice Peach

K001-1005
Aqua

Sunrise roll-up, Sunrise fat quarter bundle, and Sunrise charm pack

Palette Colors

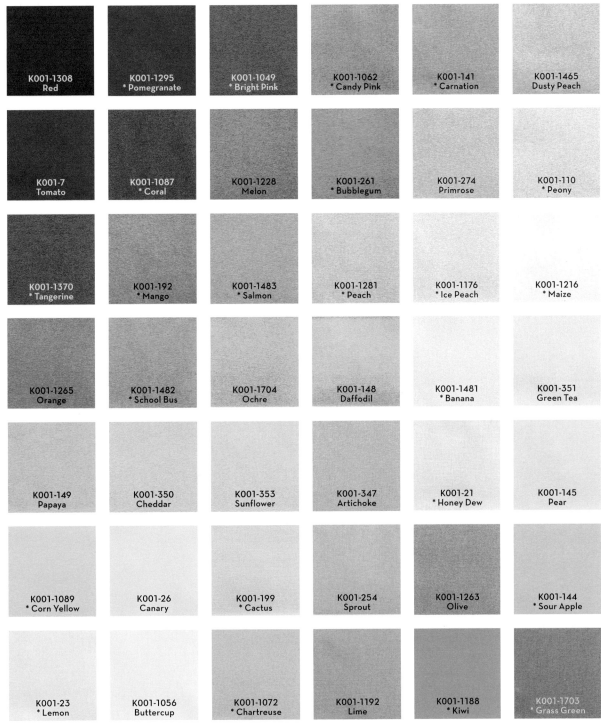

K001-1308 Red	K001-1295 * Pomegranate	K001-1049 * Bright Pink	K001-1062 * Candy Pink	K001-141 * Carnation	K001-1465 Dusty Peach
K001-7 Tomato	K001-1087 * Coral	K001-1228 Melon	K001-261 * Bubblegum	K001-274 Primrose	K001-110 * Peony
K001-1370 * Tangerine	K001-192 * Mango	K001-1483 * Salmon	K001-1281 * Peach	K001-1176 * Ice Peach	K001-1216 * Maize
K001-1265 Orange	K001-1482 * School Bus	K001-1704 Ochre	K001-148 Daffodil	K001-1481 * Banana	K001-351 Green Tea
K001-149 Papaya	K001-350 Cheddar	K001-353 Sunflower	K001-347 Artichoke	K001-21 * Honey Dew	K001-145 Pear
K001-1089 * Corn Yellow	K001-26 Canary	K001-199 * Cactus	K001-254 Sprout	K001-1263 Olive	K001-144 * Sour Apple
K001-23 * Lemon	K001-1056 Buttercup	K001-1072 * Chartreuse	K001-1192 Lime	K001-1188 * Kiwi	K001-1703 * Grass Green

Kona Sunset Palette

The Kona Sunset palette is available in charm packs and 2½″ × WOF strips in roll-ups of 42 colors. A selection of 23 of these colors (indicated by asterisks) comes in fat quarter bundles.

Suggested Backgrounds

K001-1387
White

K001-145
Pear

K001-1266
Orchid

K001-152
Cloud

K001-1003
Amethyst

K001-1010
Baby Blue

Sunset roll-up, Sunset fat quarter bundle, and Sunset charm pack

HELLO
MY NAME IS

Roll - Up
At a usable 2-1/2" x WOF (44"), I'm very functional, un-roll me, and I'm perfect for binding, sashing, inner borders, strippy quilts, strip piecing, fabric hooking, and much more!

ROBERT KAUFMAN

KONA
Charm Square

Palette Colors

K001-135 Clover	K001-1141 Fern	K001-1293 Pistachio	K001-1061 * Candy Green	K001-197 Aloe	K001-1183 * Jade Green
K001-1188 * Kiwi	K001-145 * Pear	K001-1173 Ice Frappe	K001-200 * Pond	K001-1010 * Baby Blue	K001-196 * Blue Jay
K001-144 * Sour Apple	K001-1234 Mint	K001-1005 Aqua	K001-152 * Cloud	K001-27 Cornflower	K001-357 * Lapis
K001-21 * Honey Dew	K001-1009 Azure	K001-194 Lake	K001-277 * Blueberry	K001-318 * Grapemist	K001-32 Surf
K001-1011 * Bahama Blue	K001-1514 * Robin Egg	K001-1285 Periwinkle	K001-1189 * Lavender	K001-142 Crocus	K001-1541 Deep Blue
K001-1282 * Peacock	K001-1060 Candy Blue	K001-1003 * Amethyst	K001-1214 * Magenta	K001-258 Pansy	K001-1191 Lilac
K001-1376 * Turquoise	K001-1048 * Bright Peri	K001-80 Mulberry	K001-1383 * Violet	K001-24 * Petunia	K001-134 Thistle

Kona Bright Palette

The Kona Bright palette is available in charm packs and 2½" × WOF strips in roll-ups of 41 colors.

K001-1387
White

K001-1019
Black

K001-1171
Hyacinth

K001-1055
Butter

K001-1007
Ash

K001-1173
Ice Frappe

Bright roll-up and Bright charm pack

Palette Colors

K001-1308 Red	K001-1296 Poppy	K001-1087 Coral	K001-1228 Melon	K001-1483 Salmon	K001-274 Primrose
K001-190 Camellia	K001-1295 Pomegranate	K001-410 Kumquat	K001-1265 Orange	K001-1089 Corn Yellow	K001-1141 Fern
K001-419 Azalea	K001-261 Bubble Gum	K001-1482 School Bus	K001-23 Lemon	K001-348 Asparagus	K001-197 Aloe
K001-1062 Candy Pink	K001-141 Carnation	K001-1056 Buttercup	K001-200 Pond	K001-1061 Candy Green	K001-1009 Azure
K001-110 Peony	K001-1706 Celery	K001-354 Zucchini	K001-1011 Bahama Blue	K001-405 Alegria	K001-346 Regatta
K001-199 Cactus	K001-145 Pear	K001-1293 Pistachio	K001-171 Water	K001-196 * Blue Jay	K001-1383 Violet
K001-1072 Chartreuse	K001-254 Sprout	K001-1282 Peacock	K001-357 Lapis	K001-142 Crocus	

Kona Pastel Palette

The Kona Pastel palette is available in charm packs and 2½" × WOF strips in roll-ups of 41 colors. It can be used very effectively when juxtaposed with darker and more vibrant colored backgrounds.

Suggested Backgrounds

K001-1285
Periwinkle

K001-1003
Amethyst

K001-1214
Magenta

K001-1282
Peacock

K001-197
Aloe

K001-1228
Melon

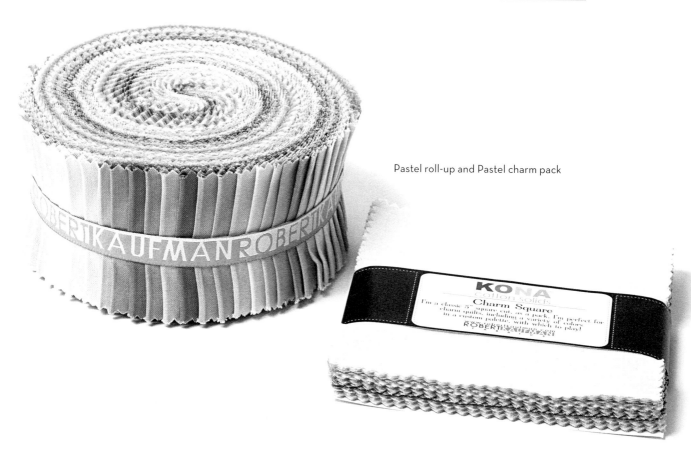

Pastel roll-up and Pastel charm pack

Palette Colors

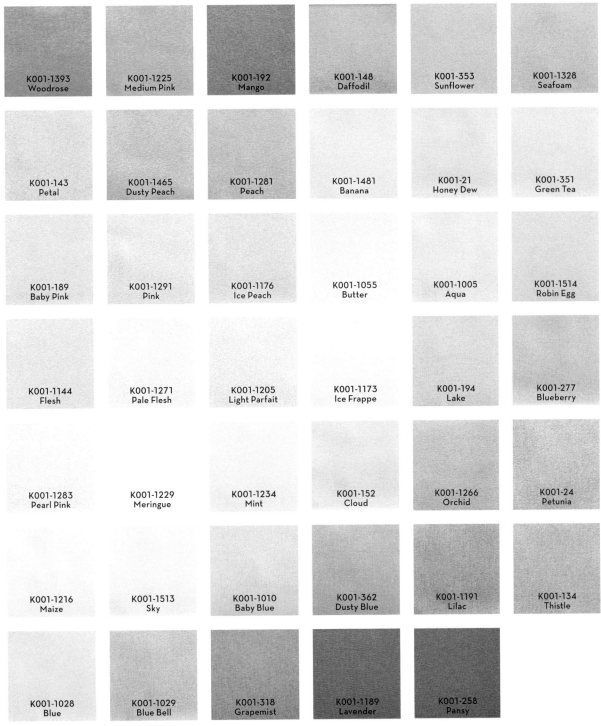

K001-1393 Woodrose	K001-1225 Medium Pink	K001-192 Mango	K001-148 Daffodil	K001-353 Sunflower	K001-1328 Seafoam
K001-143 Petal	K001-1465 Dusty Peach	K001-1281 Peach	K001-1481 Banana	K001-21 Honey Dew	K001-351 Green Tea
K001-189 Baby Pink	K001-1291 Pink	K001-1176 Ice Peach	K001-1055 Butter	K001-1005 Aqua	K001-1514 Robin Egg
K001-1144 Flesh	K001-1271 Pale Flesh	K001-1205 Light Parfait	K001-1173 Ice Frappe	K001-194 Lake	K001-277 Blueberry
K001-1283 Pearl Pink	K001-1229 Meringue	K001-1234 Mint	K001-152 Cloud	K001-1266 Orchid	K001-24 Petunia
K001-1216 Maize	K001-1513 Sky	K001-1010 Baby Blue	K001-362 Dusty Blue	K001-1191 Lilac	K001-134 Thistle
K001-1028 Blue	K001-1029 Blue Bell	K001-318 Grapemist	K001-1189 Lavender	K001-258 Pansy	

Other Kona Fat Quarter Bundles

FQ-601-21
Kona True Blue color story
21 pieces

FQ-604-22
Kona Sweet Peas color story
22 pieces

FQ-603-22
Kona Burning Up color story
22 pieces

FQ-605-22
Kona Pretty Peonies color story
22 pieces

FQ-606-22
Kona Slate Rock color story
22 pieces

FQ-608-23
Kona Farmer's Market color story
23 pieces

FQ-607-22
Kona Fields of Iris color story
22 pieces

FQ-610-23
Kona Grecian Waters color story
23 pieces

Basic Color Principles and the Work of Josef Albers

Josef Albers was a twentieth-century German-born American artist and color theorist who was active in the Bauhaus movement. His treatise *Interaction of Color* (1963) revolutionized the way color theory is taught in art schools. His series of paintings *Homage to a Square* explored the ways color influences our perception of space. By varying the intensity of hues and their arrangement and proportions, he created optical illusions that cause the viewer to perceive color differently.

Because Albers' work typically featured broad, geometric planes of color, it is particularly applicable to modern quilts that feature solid fabrics. Here are some important principles that his work explored:

1. Color is always seen in relation to the colors that surround it. Therefore, one color can appear different when placed on different backgrounds. On a light background, a medium tone might appear dark. On a dark background, that same tone might appear to be light. This same principle holds true when you throw color into the mix. For instance, a gray might appear to have a yellowish cast when placed on a cool background, while it might appear to have a bluish cast when placed on a warm background.

2. Likewise, two or more different colors can be made to appear the same by placing them on different backgrounds.

3. Dark squares nested within progressively lightening larger squares will recede in space and give the illusion of three dimensions. Different proportions and different colors vary the perception of depth.

4. Solid colors can be used to create the illusion of transparency.

5. Two hues of similar value (that would appear to be the same shade of gray if photocopied in black and white), when placed next to each other, can create a boundary that appears to vibrate.

As you work with the wonderful palette of cottons available to quilters today, keep these principles in mind. The smaller projects in this book give you a chance to explore these principles further. Albers' students worked with silk-screened papers that displayed fantastic color depth. Buy a few Kona charm packs and keep them on hand to cut up so you can explore color on a smaller scale!

Neutral Colors

The most obvious colors for neutral backgrounds are black and white, but other colors can also function as neutrals. To find a color that works as a neutral, lay out all the block colors and audition fabrics next to them to see what might work. Often a light color in the same range is effective. Other times a dark color in that range can work well, but be sure to choose a color that isn't too bright or it will overwhelm the other fabrics.

Examples of good neutral color choices

Poison Colors

Poison colors are those that are directly opposite on the color wheel from the main color scheme. They provide added interest and movement to a design. Read more about poison colors on page 15.

Examples of poison colors that I frequently use

An Added Challenge

Challenge yourself to move outside your comfort zone and away from your favorite colors. Perhaps even try to work with a color you aren't normally drawn toward. I naturally tend to steer away from working with orange in isolation; however, I do use orange in many of my fabric designs as an accent color. If you feel uncomfortable working with a hue that might be unusual for you, perhaps use it as a poison color in contrast with the main color scheme.

COLOR ESSENTIALS—Crisp & Vibrant Quilts

TRY IT!

Challenge yourself by creating a small quilted piece with color as its focus. Any of these projects is a great place to start. See Quiltmaking Basics (page 140) for added tips and techniques.

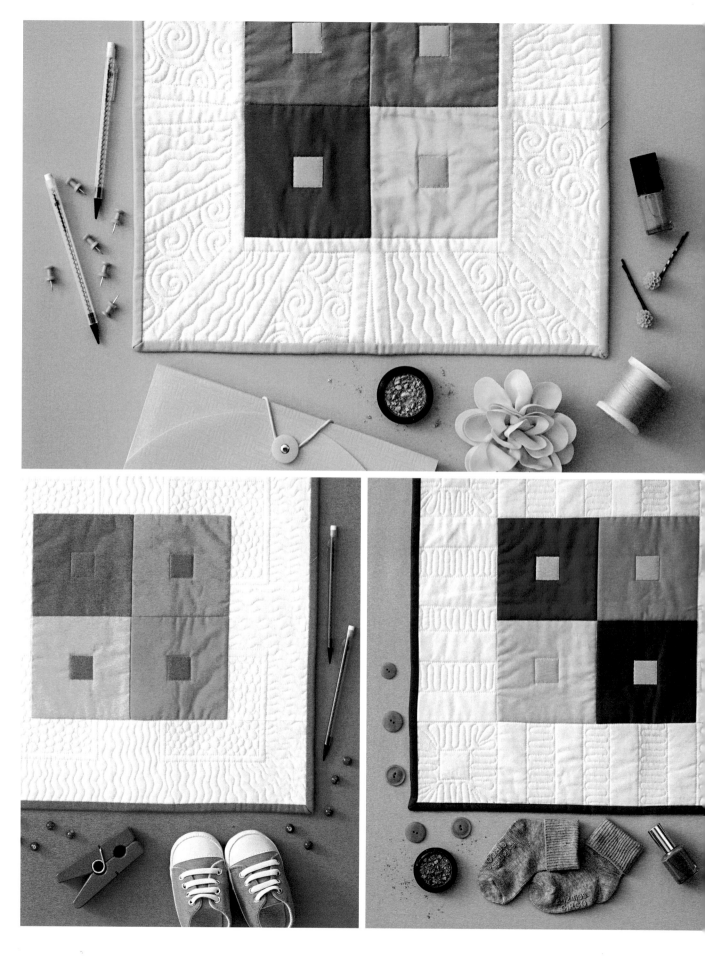

Making One Color Look Like More:
Illusion Pillow

Practice making one piece of fabric appear slightly different in hue by changing the surrounding background color. Be sure to read the color information (page 30) prior to starting this project.

Assorted Illusion Pillows—Bright palette

Pieced and quilted by Amanda Murphy

MATERIALS
FOR 1 PILLOW

BLOCKS: 1 Kona Sunrise, Sunset, or Bright charm pack (You will have extra charms left over.)

BACKGROUND FABRIC: 3/8 yard Kona 1387 White

PILLOW BACK FABRIC: 5/8 yard

BINDING FABRIC: 1/4 yard

CONTRASTING BUTTONHOLE PANEL FABRIC:
1 rectangle 4¾" × 18"

MUSLIN: 18" × 18" square

BATTING: 18" × 18" square (I like Warm & Natural batting by the Warm Company.)

PAPER-BACKED FUSIBLE WEB: 1 small piece, approximately 5" × 5"

TEAR-AWAY STABILIZER (*OPTIONAL*):
1 small piece, approximately 4" × 4"
(I like Sulky Tear-Easy.)

3 BUTTONS 1" IN DIAMETER

FUSIBLE INTERFACING: 2 strips 2" × 18"

16" × 16" PILLOW FORM

CUTTING
INSTRUCTIONS

WOF = width of fabric

FROM BACKGROUND FABRIC
- Cut 2 strips 4½" × WOF. Subcut 2 rectangles 4½" × 9½" and 2 rectangles 4½" × 17½".

FROM PILLOW BACK FABRIC
- Cut 1 rectangle 7" × 18" and 1 rectangle 13" × 18".

FROM BINDING FABRIC
- Cut 2 strips 2¼" × WOF.

Pillow Top Assembly

Use a ¼" seam allowance unless noted otherwise.

1. Select 1 Kona charm square and back it with paper-backed fusible web. Cut into 4 squares 1" × 1". (If you feel unsure about color for this exercise, choosing a gray is a great place to start.)

2. Audition each 1" square on top of other colored charm squares. Find combinations in which the small squares take on a different look because of their backgrounds. (Try warm and cool combinations, light and dark combinations, etc.) When you are satisfied, remove the paper backing and fuse the small squares onto the middle of 4 different backgrounds. Appliqué in matching thread to secure.

3. Join the blocks into a 4-square unit.
FIGURE A

4. Following the assembly diagram, join a border rectangle 4½″ × 9½″ to each side of the 4-square unit.

5. Join background rectangles 4½″ × 17½″ to the top and bottom of the block. FIGURE B

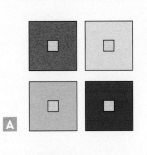

A

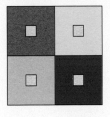

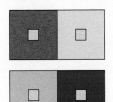

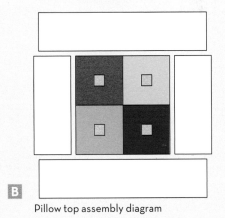

B

Pillow top assembly diagram

6. Spread out a piece of muslin or scrap fabric that is at least 18″ × 18″ square. (You won't see it in the finished pillow.) Spread a piece of the same size batting on top. Smooth the pillow top *right side up* on top of the batting and muslin and quilt as desired. There are many ways to echo the square shapes of the center motif in the background area of the pillow. Have fun!

7. Trim the quilted pillow top to 16½″ × 16½″.

Finishing

1. Join the long edge of the buttonhole panel rectangle 4¾″ × 18″ to the long edge of the pillow back rectangle 7″ × 18″. Turn the other long edge of the buttonhole panel under ½″ and press. Fold the buttonhole panel under again lengthwise, wrong sides together, so that the folded edge meets the seam. Press. Open up the folds and slipstitch an interfacing strip into the buttonhole panel. Press to fuse the interfacing. Pin.

2. Turn the entire unit right side up and topstitch along the buttonhole panel with matching thread, ⅛″ below the seam between the 2 pieces of fabric. This will secure the folded edge on the wrong side as well.

3. Sew 1 buttonhole in the center of the buttonhole panel and another 3¾" out from each side of the center buttonhole.

4. Turn 1 long edge of the large pillow back rectangle 13" × 18" under ½" and press. Turn the same side under 2" and press. Open up the folds and slipstitch an interfacing strip into this fold and press to fuse.

5. Turn this unit wrong side up and topstitch ⅛" from the edge of the first fold to secure.

6. Baste the top and bottom units together as shown, so that the edge of the top unit just overlaps the topstitching on the bottom unit. Open up the buttonholes and mark the button placement on the bottom panel. **FIGURE C**

7. Layer the quilted pillow top onto the back, *wrong sides together,* and baste ⅛" from the pillow top edge. Trim excess pillow back fabric.

8. Join together the binding strips. Fold in half lengthwise and press. Sew the binding by machine to the outer edge of the pillow front, through all the layers. Wrap the binding around to the pillow back and hand stitch to secure. Remove the basting from the back panel and apply the buttons. Enjoy your lovely pillow!

Baste.

C

Pillow back diagram

Making Colors Vibrate:
Table Runner

Pick two colors of the same value on opposite sides of the color wheel and experiment with making color vibrate! This can even work with two hues that are closer together on the color wheel as long as you stick with colors of similar value. It is also fun to make this project in two contrasting colors and let the quilting take center stage!

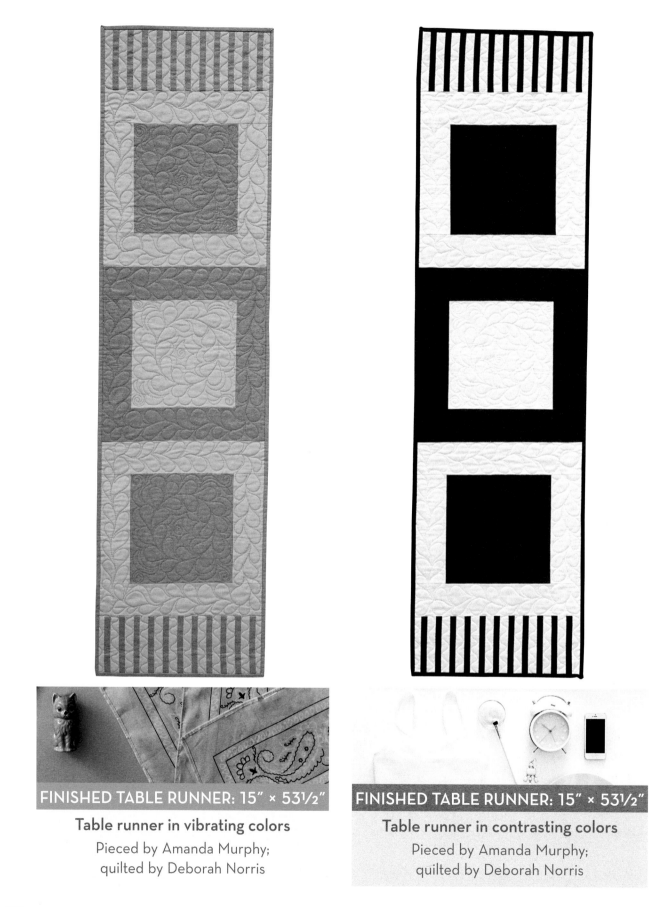

FINISHED TABLE RUNNER: 15" × 53½"

Table runner in vibrating colors

Pieced by Amanda Murphy;
quilted by Deborah Norris

FINISHED TABLE RUNNER: 15" × 53½"

Table runner in contrasting colors

Pieced by Amanda Murphy;
quilted by Deborah Norris

MATERIALS

RUNNER FABRIC A: ¾ yard Kona 1011 Bahama Blue (or 1387 White)

RUNNER FABRIC B: ¾ yard Kona 192 Mango (or 1019 Black)

BACKING FABRIC: 1 yard Kona 1011 Bahama Blue (or 1387 White)

BINDING FABRIC: ⅓ yard Kona 192 Mango (or 1019 Black)

BATTING: 18″ × 57″ (I like Warm & Natural batting by the Warm Company.)

PAPER-BACKED FUSIBLE TAPE, ¼″-WIDE: 4 yards (I like Lite Steam-A-Seam 2.)

½″ FUSIBLE BIAS TAPE MAKER (optional, but very helpful)

CUTTING
INSTRUCTIONS   WOF = width of fabric

FROM FABRIC A (BAHAMA BLUE)

• Cut 3 strips 3¼″ × WOF. Subcut into 4 rectangles 3¼″ × 9½″ and 4 rectangles 3¼″ × 15″.

• Cut 1 strip 5½″ × WOF. Subcut into 2 rectangles 5½″ × 16″.

• Cut 1 strip 9½″ × WOF. Subcut into 1 square 9½″ × 9½″.

FROM FABRIC B (MANGO)

• Cut 2 strips 3¼″ × WOF. Subcut into 2 rectangles 3¼″ × 9½″ and 2 rectangles 3¼″ × 15″.

• Cut 4 strips 1″ × WOF.

• Cut 1 strip 9½″ × WOF. Subcut into 2 squares 9½″ × 9½″.

FROM BACKING FABRIC

• Cut 2 strips 18″ × WOF.

FROM BINDING FABRIC

• Cut 4 strips 2¼″ × WOF.

Block Assembly

Use a ¼" seam allowance unless noted otherwise.

1. Join fabric A rectangles 3¼" × 9½" to the top and bottom of a fabric B square 9½" × 9½". Join fabric A rectangles 3¼" × 15" to both sides of this unit. Repeat to make a second unit. **FIGURE A**

2. Join fabric B rectangles 3¼" × 9½" to the top and bottom of a fabric A square 9½" × 9½". Join fabric B rectangles 3¼" × 15" to both sides of this unit. **FIGURE B**

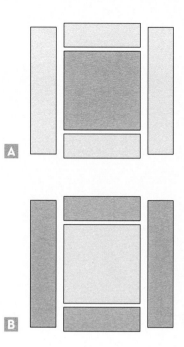

Border Assembly

1. Run 1" fabric B strips and ¼"-wide fusible tape through a fusible bias tape maker, following the product instructions. If you don't have a fusible bias tape maker, fold the fabric B strips lengthwise wrong sides together, so that the edges meet in the center of the strip. Fuse to the wrong (folded) side of the fabric B strips; *then* remove the paper backing.

2. Cut the strips into 22 segments 6½" in length.

3. Starting 1½″ in from the short edge of a fabric A rectangle 5½″ × 16″, fuse 11 fabric B segments at even intervals ¾″ apart, allowing the edges of the segments to overlap the fabric A rectangle. **FIGURE C**

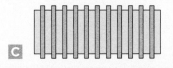

4. Secure the segments using an invisible hem stitch in matching thread.

5. Trim the edges of the segments flush with the border rectangle. **FIGURE D**

6. Centering the segments, trim the border to a rectangle 5½″ × 15″.

7. Repeat Steps 3–6 to make another border.

Runner Assembly

Following the assembly diagram, join the blocks and borders to form the runner.

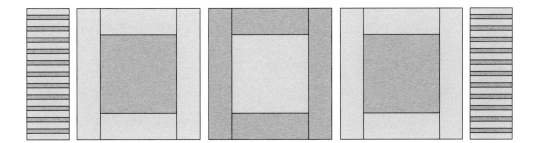

Finishing

1. Sew the short ends of the 2 backing fabric pieces together, press, and trim to a rectangle 18″ × 57″.

2. Layer the backing, batting, and runner top. Baste. Quilt as desired.

3. See Binding (page 141) to make the binding and bind the runner.

Transparency:
Place Mats

Choose analogous hues from a cool or warm palette and piece them into an interlocking pattern. Thoughtful placement gives the illusion of transparency.

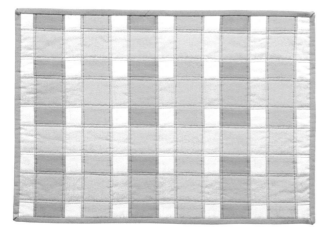

FINISHED PLACE MAT: 19" × 13"

Place mats whose colors give the illusion of transparent overlays of sheer fabrics

Pieced and quilted by Amanda Murphy

MATERIALS
FOR 4 PLACE MATS

BLOCK PATTERN (AQUA): 2 Kona Sunrise or Sunset roll-ups (or 1 of each!)

BACKGROUND FABRIC: ⅝ yard Kona 1387 White

BACKING FABRIC: 1 yard Kona 1007 Ash

BINDING FABRIC: ⅝ yard

BATTING: 1 yard, 45″ wide (I like Warm & Natural batting by the Warm Company.)

FROM THE ROLL-UP:

Choose 2 shades of 1 color, say, green, and 2 shades of an analogous color, like aqua, from your roll-up. We'll call these fabrics Green 1 (G1) and Green 2 (G2) and Aqua 1 (A1) and Aqua 2 (A2).

Now find 4 more colors that represent the mix of Green 1 with Aqua 1 (G1/A1), Green 1 with Aqua 2 (G1/A2), Green 2 with Aqua 1 (G2/A1), and Green 2 with Aqua 2 (G2/A2). *You may have to try a variety of color combinations to find something you are satisfied with.*

You will need 1 strip of each color for 1 place mat.

You will piece 1 place mat at a time.

CUTTING
INSTRUCTIONS FOR 1 PLACE MAT

WOF = width of fabric

FROM BACKGROUND FABRIC
• Cut 3 strips 1½″ × WOF. Cut each in half to form 2 rectangles 1½″ × 20″. You will use 5 rectangles and have 1 extra rectangle.

FROM ROLL-UP STRIPS
• Cut strips G1 and G2 in half to form rectangles 2½″ × 20″.

• Cut down strips A1 and A2 to a width of 1½″. Subcut each strip into 5 rectangles 1½″ × 8″.

• Cut each A1/G1, A2/G1, A1/G2, and A2/G2 strip into 2 rectangles 2½″ × 8″.

FROM BACKING FABRIC
• Cut 1 rectangle 14″ × 20″.

FROM BINDING FABRIC
• Cut 2 strips 2¼″ × WOF (or use 2 matching strips from the roll-ups).

FROM BATTING
• Cut 1 rectangle 14″ × 20″.

Strip Set Piecing

Use a ¼" seam allowance unless noted otherwise.

Strip Set A

1. Join 2 G1 strips, 2 G2 strips, and 5 background strips as shown and press the seams away from the background fabric. **FIGURE A**

2. Cut 7 units 1½" wide from the strip set.
FIGURE B

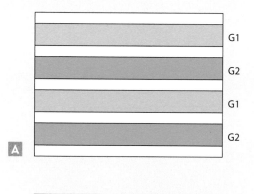

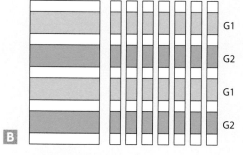

Strip Set B

1. Join 2 A1/G1 rectangles, 2 A1/G2 rectangles, and 5 A1 rectangles as shown and press the seams toward the A1 fabric. **FIGURE C**

2. Cut 3 units 2½" wide from the strip set.
FIGURE D

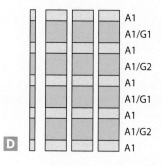

Strip Set C

1. Join 2 A2/G1 rectangles, 2 A2/G2 rectangles, and 5 A2 rectangles as shown and press the seams toward the A2 fabric. **FIGURE E**

2. Cut 3 units 2½" wide from the strip set. **FIGURE F**

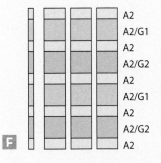

E | A2
A2/G1
A2
A2/G2
A2
A2/G1
A2
A2/G2
A2

F | A2
A2/G1
A2
A2/G2
A2
A2/G1
A2
A2/G2
A2

Place Mat Assembly

1. Following the assembly diagram, lay out the columns cut from the strip sets to create the illusion of transparency. **FIGURE G**

2. Join the columns and press the seams open. **FIGURE H**

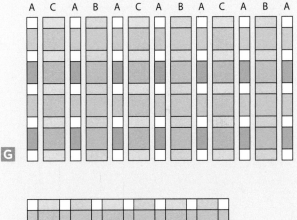

A C A B A C A B A C A B A

G

Finishing

1. Layer the backing, batting, and place mat top. Baste. Quilt as desired.

2. See Binding (page 141) to make the binding and bind the place mat.

Repeat the cutting, strip set piecing, and assembly steps to make the remaining 3 place mats.

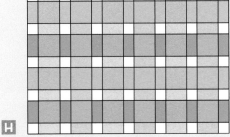

H

The HEART of the Matter

Explore color theory on a larger scale with these projects. Whether you prefer appliqué or like to piece, you are sure to find something here to fit your personal style! Use the Robert Kaufman precuts (pages 16–29) as a starting point for your palette. Be sure to carefully consider the background color choice, as it can have an enormous impact on the overall look of the project. Most importantly, have fun!

City Lights

Let your favorite solid precuts illuminate this quilt. Instructions are for the Sunset color palette. To sew the Bright version, substitute a Kona Bright roll-up and charm packs for the Sunset precuts, and use Kona 1019 Black for the background fabric, Kona 1282 Peacock for the binding, and Kona 353 Sunflower for the backing fabric.

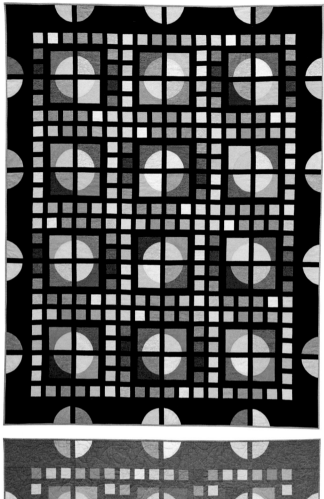

City Lights—Bright palette

Pieced by Amanda Murphy;
quilted by Deborah Norris

City Lights—Sunset palette

Pieced by Amanda Murphy;
quilted by Deborah Norris

The quilting pattern is
Interlocking Shooting Stars,
copyright © 2000 by Bonnie Borseth.

MATERIALS

BLOCK FABRICS: 1 Kona Sunset roll-up (select 20 strips) and 4 Kona Sunset charm packs (select 31 charm squares from each—124 total)

BACKGROUND FABRIC: 4 yards Kona 1003 Amethyst

BINDING FABRIC: ⅝ yard Kona 258 Pansy

BACKING FABRIC: 5¼ yards Kona 1189 Lavender or 1005 Aqua

TEAR-AWAY STABILIZER, 20" WIDE: 2 yards (I like Sulky Tear-Easy.)

BATTING: 72" × 90" (I like Warm & Natural batting by the Warm Company.)

PAPER-BACKED FUSIBLE WEB, 24" WIDE: 3 yards (I like Lite Steam-A-Seam.)

APPLIQUÉ THREAD, 28 WEIGHT: a variety of colors

CUTTING
INSTRUCTIONS   WOF = width of fabric

FROM BACKGROUND FABRIC

• Cut 20 strips 1½" × WOF.

• Cut 10 more strips 1½" × WOF. Piece into 3 rectangles 1½" × 53½". Subcut remaining strips into 24 rectangles 1½" × 5" and 12 rectangles 1½" × 10½".

• Cut 16 strips 2" × WOF. Subcut into 24 rectangles 2" × 10½" and 24 rectangles 2" × 13½".

• Cut 3 strips 6" × WOF. Subcut into 4 rectangles 6" × 14", 4 rectangles 6" × 8½", and 14 rectangles 6" × 1½".

• Cut 2 strips 17½" × WOF. Subcut into 10 rectangles 6" × 17½" and 8 rectangles 1½" × 17½".

FROM BINDING FABRIC

• Cut 8 strips 2¼" × WOF.

FROM FUSIBLE WEB

• Cut 76 squares 5" × 5".

FROM TEAR-AWAY STABILIZER

• Cut 76 squares 4" × 4".

Block Assembly

Small Squares Strip Sets

1. Join 4 roll-up strips with 5 background strips 1½″ × WOF, beginning and ending with a background strip. (You can vary the color arrangement or create a gradation as shown.) Repeat to form a second strip set, this time using different colored strips. Cut a total of 24 units 2½″ wide from these sets. These are the 4-square units. **FIGURE A**

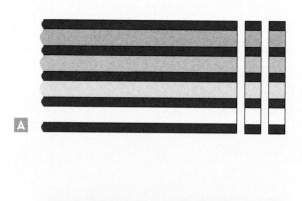

2. Join 6 roll-up strips with 5 background strips 1½″ × WOF, beginning and ending with a rol- up strip. (You can vary the color arrangement or create a gradation as shown.) Repeat to form a second strip set, this time using different colored strips. You can choose to arrange your colors in an ordered fashion as I did in my quilt, or you can randomly place the strips for a less controlled look. Cut a total of 24 units 2½″ wide from these sets. These are the 6-square units. **FIGURE B**

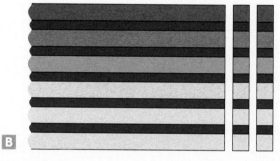

Center Circle Blocks

1. Select 48 charm squares for the background of the quarter-circle units. Set aside.

2. Refer to Fusible Appliqué (page 63) to trace Pattern A onto the smooth side of 76 paper-backed fusible web squares 5″ × 5″. Trim excess fusible web along the inner (solid line) curve so your finished quilt will not be stiff, making sure to leave at least a ¼″ margin of fusible web remaining.

3. Fuse a Pattern A shape onto each of the 76 remaining charm squares, aligning the raw edges with the corners.

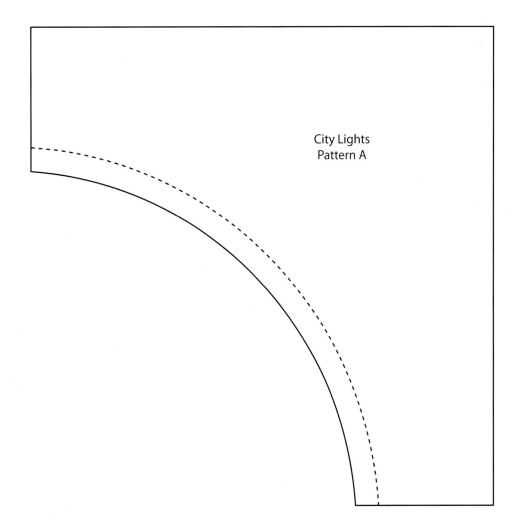

City Lights
Pattern A

4. Cut out the quarter-circles along the dashed lines. Remove the paper and fuse 1 quarter-circle onto each of the charm squares set aside earlier, aligning the raw edges as shown. (You will have 28 quarter-circles remaining.) **FIGURE C**

5. Refer to Fusible Appliqué (page 63) to chain appliqué the curved edges of the quarter-circles, backing with tear-away stabilizer and using a blanket stitch with thick, contrasting threads. (You don't have to worry about knotting the ends of the threads, as they will be caught in the seams.) Remove the stabilizer from the back of the blocks and cut away excess background fabric from behind each quarter-circle.

6. Join 2 quarter-circle blocks with a background rectangle 1½" × 5". Repeat to make 24 units. **FIGURE D**

7. Join 2 of these half-circle units with a background rectangle 1½" × 10½". Repeat to make 12 full-circle units. **FIGURE E**

8. Join background rectangles 2" × 10½" to both sides of each of the full-circle units. **FIGURE F**

9. Join background rectangles 2" × 13½" to the top and bottom of each of the full-circle units. **FIGURE G**

10. Join a 4-square unit to each side of each of the full-circle units. **FIGURE H**

11. Join 6-square units to the top and bottom of each of the full-circle units. **FIGURE I**

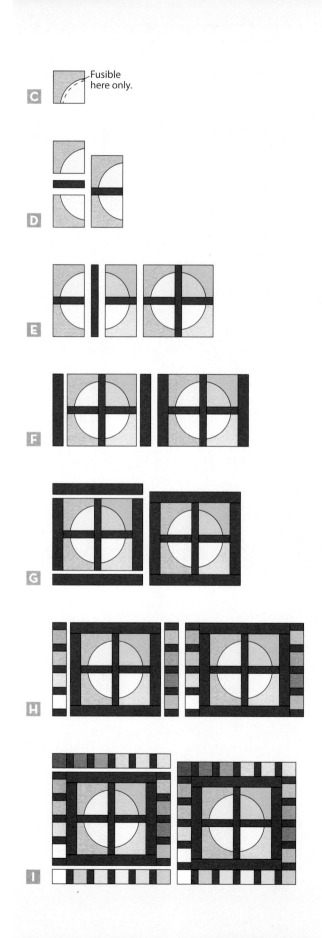

Fusible here only.

Fusible Appliqué

1. Trace the appliqué shape onto the smooth side of the paper-backed fusible web. Cut excess fusible web from inside the shape. **FIGURE A**

2. Fuse to the back of the appliqué fabric. **FIGURE B**

3. Cut out the appliqué along the dashed line and remove the paper. **FIGURE C**

4. Following the manufacturer's instructions, fuse onto the block. **FIGURE D**

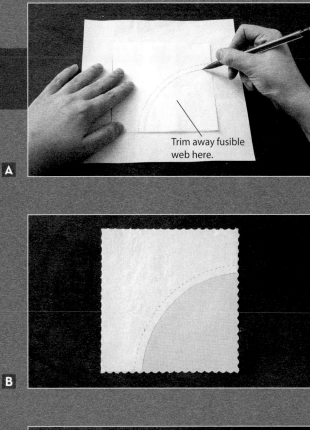

Trim away fusible web here.

A

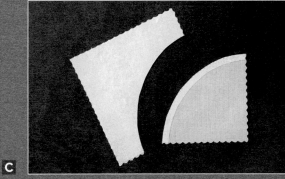

B

C

D

5. After fusing the shapes in place, back the block with tear-away stabilizer. For a fun, professional-looking finish, use a heavyweight contrasting thread, like Aurifil's 12- or 28-weight or Sulky's 12- or 30-weight cotton, with a large top-stitching needle when securing fusible appliqué shapes to your project.

6. Choose a blanket-style stitch (#1329 on the Bernina 580e) and loosen the thread tension so the bobbin thread does not pop to the top of the piece if you choose to use a lighter-weight thread in the bottom. *Note: If your machine doesn't have a blanket-style stitch, you can use a narrow zigzag stitch with a lighter-weight thread.* Bring both threads to the top of the fabric. While holding them to the side, begin to sew around the shape. **FIGURE E**

7. After reaching the end point, lift the presser foot and pull the piece out from the machine. Clip the threads so the tails are about 4" long. **FIGURE F**

Note: If your appliqué stitches will be caught in the seam, as in the City Lights blocks, skip Steps 7–9 here, and simply clip the threads, leaving the tails about ½" long.

8. Thread all the tails into a chenille needle with a large eye and bring them to the back of the block. Tie a knot close to the fabric. **FIGURE G**

9. Rip off the stabilizer and trim excess fabric from the back of the appliqué to get rid of the bulk. **FIGURE H**

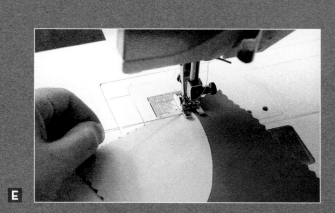

E

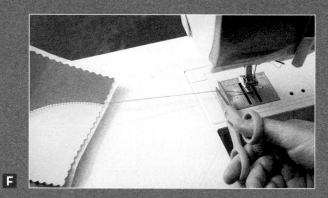

F

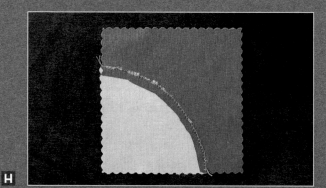

G

H

Border Blocks

1. Remove the paper from the remaining quarter-circles and fuse quarter-circles onto the right bottom corners of 2 background rectangles 6″ × 14″. Fuse quarter-circles onto the left bottom corners of the remaining 2 background rectangles 6″ × 14″. **FIGURE J**

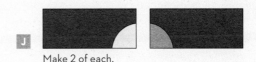

J

Make 2 of each.

2. Fuse quarter-circles onto the right bottom corners of 2 background rectangles 6″ × 8½″. Fuse quarter-circles onto the left bottom corners of the remaining 2 background rectangles 6″ × 8½″. **FIGURE K**

K

Make 2 of each.

3. Fuse quarter-circles onto *both* bottom corners of all the background rectangles 6″ × 17½″. **FIGURE L**

L

Make 10.

4. Refer to Fusible Appliqué, Steps 5–7 (page 64), to chain appliqué the curved edges of the border block quarter-circles. You don't have to worry about knotting the ends of the threads, as they will be caught in the seams.

5. Join 3 border blocks 6″ × 17½″ with 2 border blocks 6″ × 8½″ and 4 background rectangles 1½″ × 6″ as shown in the assembly diagram (page 66) to form a side border. Repeat to make another side border.

6. Join 2 border blocks 6″ × 17½″ with 2 border blocks 6″ × 14″ and 3 background rectangles 1½″ × 6″ as shown in the assembly diagram (page 66) to form the top border. Repeat to make the bottom border.

Quilt Assembly

1. Following the assembly diagram, join 3 circle blocks with 2 background rectangles 1½″ × 17½″ to form a row. Repeat to make 4 rows.

2. Continuing to follow the assembly diagram, join the circle block rows with 3 background rectangles 1½″ × 53½″ to form the center of the quilt top.

3. Join the side borders to the quilt top.

4. Join the top and bottom borders to the quilt top.

Assembly diagram

Finishing

1. Divide the backing fabric into 2 equal lengths. Cut 1 piece lengthwise to make 2 narrow panels. Join 1 narrow panel to each side of the wide panel. Press the seams open.

2. Layer the backing, batting, and quilt top. Baste. Quilt as desired.

3. See Binding (page 141) to make the binding and bind the quilt.

COLOR POSSIBILITIES

Sunset on 21 Honeydew

Pastel on 1061 Candy Green

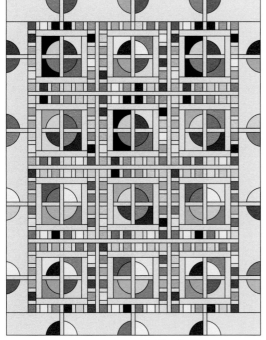

Sunset on 152 Cloud

Pastel on 1055 Butter

Stairways

Use a roll-up to create a dynamic stairway of color! Quilting a cascading design on each stair adds a special touch.

FINISHED QUILT: 56" × 72"

Stairways—Bright palette

Pieced by Amanda Murphy;
quilted by Deborah Norris

MATERIALS

BLOCK FABRICS: 1 Kona Bright roll-up (or 23 strips 2½″ wide)

BACKGROUND FABRIC: 2½ yards Kona 1387 White

INNER BORDER FABRIC: ⅓ yard Kona 1370 Tangerine

OUTER BORDER FABRIC: 1 yard Kona 1514 Robin Egg

BINDING FABRIC: ⅝ yard Kona 1514 Robin Egg

BACKING FABRIC: 4¾ yards Kona 1265 Orange

BATTING: 64″ × 80″ (I like Warm & White batting by the Warm Company.)

CUTTING
INSTRUCTIONS WOF = width of fabric

FROM ROLL-UPS
- Cut 21 rectangles 2½″ × 10½″, 23 rectangles 2½″ × 8½″, 2 rectangles 2½″ × 6½″, 2 rectangles 2½″ × 4½″, and 102 squares 2½″ × 2½″.

FROM BACKGROUND FABRIC
- Cut 29 strips 2½″ × WOF.

- Set 6 strips aside for the background border. Subcut the remaining strips into 1 rectangle 2½″ × 10½″, 45 rectangles 2½″ × 8½″, 4 rectangles 2½″ × 6½″, 48 rectangles 2½″ × 4½″, and 41 squares 2½″ × 2½″.

FROM INNER BORDER FABRIC
- Cut 6 strips 1½″ × WOF.

FROM OUTER BORDER FABRIC
- Cut 7 strips 4¼″ × WOF.

FROM BINDING FABRIC
- Cut 8 strips 2¼″ × WOF.

Block Assembly

Use a ¼" seam allowance unless noted otherwise.

Preparation

1. Draw a diagonal line on the back of each background square 2½" × 2½".

2. With the diagonal line oriented as shown, place a background square 2½" × 2½" on top of each of 18 roll-up rectangles 2½" × 8½" and 20 roll-up rectangles 2½" × 10½". Sew directly on the diagonal lines. Trim the seam allowances to ¼" and press them toward the background corners.
FIGURE A

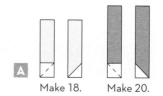

Make 18.   Make 20.

3. With the diagonal line oriented as shown, place a background square 2½" × 2½" on top of 1 roll-up rectangle 2½" × 4½" and 1 roll-up rectangle 2½" × 6½". Sew directly on the diagonal line. Trim the seam allowances to ¼" and press them toward the background corners. **FIGURE B**

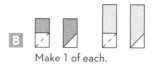

Make 1 of each.

4. Join 2 roll-up squares 2½" × 2½" together to make a 2-square unit. Press the seams toward the darker fabric. Repeat to make 50 units. Set 2 of these units aside. (There will be 2 squares 2½" × 2½" left over.) **FIGURE C**

5. Join 2 of the 2-square units together to make a four-patch. Repeat to make 24 four-patches.
FIGURE D

Full Block (Make 17)

1. Join a background rectangle 2½″ × 4½″ to each side of a four-patch and press the seams toward the four-patch. Join background rectangles 2½″ × 8½″ to the top and bottom of this unit and press the seams toward the center. Repeat to make 22 of these units. (Set 5 aside to use for partial blocks.) **FIGURES E-F**

2. Join a pieced 2½″ × 8½″ unit to the bottom of a full four-patch block as shown. **FIGURE G**

3. Join a pieced 2½″ × 10½″ unit to the left side of the full four-patch block. **FIGURE H**

4. Repeat Steps 2 and 3 to make a total of 17 full blocks.

Partial Block A (Make 4)

Join roll-up rectangles 2½″ × 8½″ to the left sides of 4 of the units set aside in Full Block, Step 1. **FIGURE I**

Partial Block B (Make 1)

Join a pieced rectangle 2½″ × 8½″ to the bottom of 1 unit set aside in Full Block, Step 1. **FIGURE J**

Partial Block C (Make 1)

1. Join a roll-up square 2½″ × 2½″ to a background rectangle 2½″ × 8½″. **FIGURE K**

2. Join this unit to a pieced 2½″ × 10½″ unit. **FIGURE L**

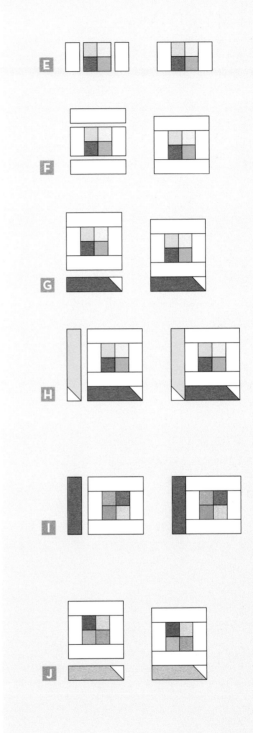

Partial Block D (Make 1)

1. Join a background rectangle 2½″ × 4½″ to the right side *only* of a four-patch and press the seams toward the four-patch. Join background rectangles 2½″ × 6½″ to the top and bottom of this unit and press the seams toward the center. **FIGURE M**

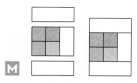

2. Join a pieced 2½″ × 6½″ unit to the bottom of the block. **FIGURE N**

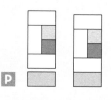

Partial Block E (Make 1)

1. Join a background rectangle 2½″ × 4½″ to the left side of a 2-square unit and press the seams toward the 2-square unit. Join background rectangles 2½″ × 4½″ to the top and bottom of this unit and press the seams toward the center. **FIGURE O**

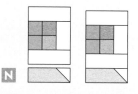

2. Join a roll-up rectangle 2½″ × 4½″ unit to the bottom of the block. **FIGURE P**

3. Join a 2½″ × 10½″ unit to the left side of the block as shown. **FIGURE Q**

Partial Block F (Make 1)

1. Join a background rectangle 2½″ × 4½″ to the right side of a 2-square unit and press the seams toward the 2-square unit. Join background rectangles 2½″ × 4½″ to the top and bottom of this unit and press the seams toward the center. **FIGURE R**

2. Join a pieced 2½″ × 4½″ unit to the bottom of the block as shown. **FIGURE S**

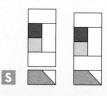

Partial Block G (Make 1)

1. Join a background rectangle 2½" × 4½" to the left side of a four-patch and press the seam toward the four-patch. Join background rectangles 2½" × 6½" to the top and bottom of this unit and press the seams toward the center. **FIGURE T**

2. Join a roll-up rectangle 2½" × 6½" to the bottom of the block. **FIGURE U**

3. Join a pieced 2½" × 10½" unit to the left side of the block. **FIGURE V**

Partial Block H (Make 2)

1. Draw a diagonal line from corner to corner on the back of a roll-up square 2½" × 2½". Place the square on top of a background rectangle 2½" × 10½" as shown. Sew directly on the diagonal line. Trim the seams to ¼" and press toward the corner. **FIGURE W**

2. Repeat with a background square 2½" × 2½" and a roll-up rectangle 2½" × 10½". **FIGURE X**

Quilt Assembly

1. Following the assembly diagram (page 76), arrange the full and partial blocks to form the center of the quilt top. The bottom row will need 1 additional roll-up rectangle 2½" × 8½" sewn to the last block on the right to complete the pattern.

2. Join the blocks into rows and press the seams away from the background fabric.

3. Join the rows and press the seams upward.

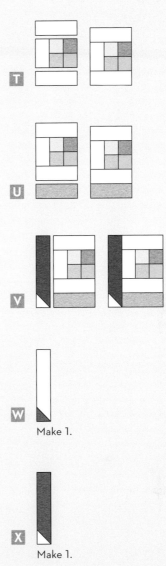

Make 1.

Make 1.

My quilt top at this point measured 42½" × 58½". Measure your quilt in both directions through the center and adjust the border measurements that follow if needed.

4. Piece 2 rectangles 2½" × 58½" from the 2½" × WOF background strips. Join to each side of the quilt top. Piece 2 rectangles 2½" × 46½" from the remaining 2½" × WOF background strips and join to the top and bottom of the quilt top.

5. Piece 2 inner border rectangles 1½" × 62½" and join to each side of the quilt top. Piece 2 inner border rectangles 1½" × 48½" and join to the top and bottom of the quilt top.

6. Piece 2 outer border rectangles 4¼" × 64½" and join to each side of the quilt top. Piece 2 outer border rectangles 4¼" × 56" and join to the top and bottom of the quilt top.

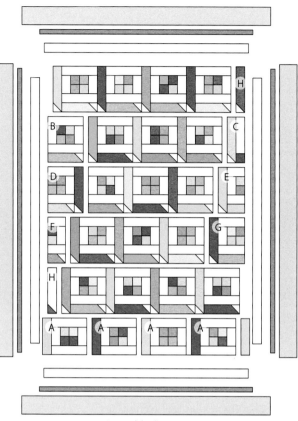

Assembly diagram

Finishing

1. Divide the backing fabric into 2 lengths. Cut 1 piece lengthwise to make 2 narrow panels. Join 1 narrow panel to each side of the wide panel. Press the seams open.

2. Layer the backing, batting, and quilt top. Baste. Quilt as desired.

3. See Binding (page 141) to make the binding and bind the quilt.

COLOR POSSIBILITIES

Pastel on 1263 Navy

Bright on 1387 White

Pastel on 351 Green Tea

Sunset on 1019 Black

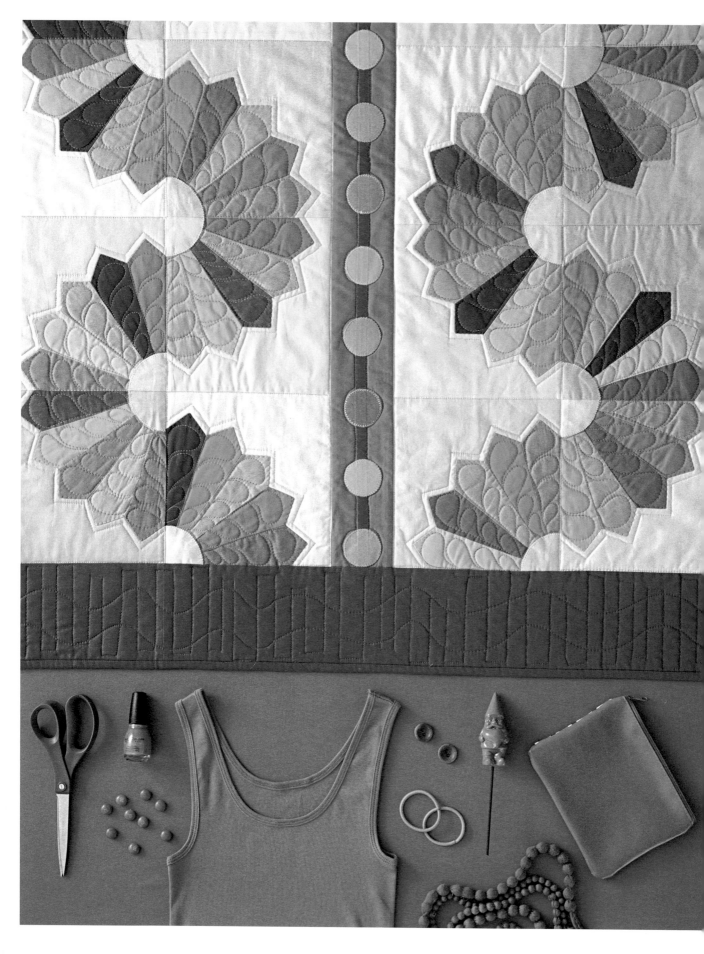

Lollipop

This modern adaptation of a Dresden Plate is eye-catching on a twin bed! Adding columns makes it easily adaptable for a queen or king. Choose a few of your favorite fat quarter bundles—there are so many color possibilities!

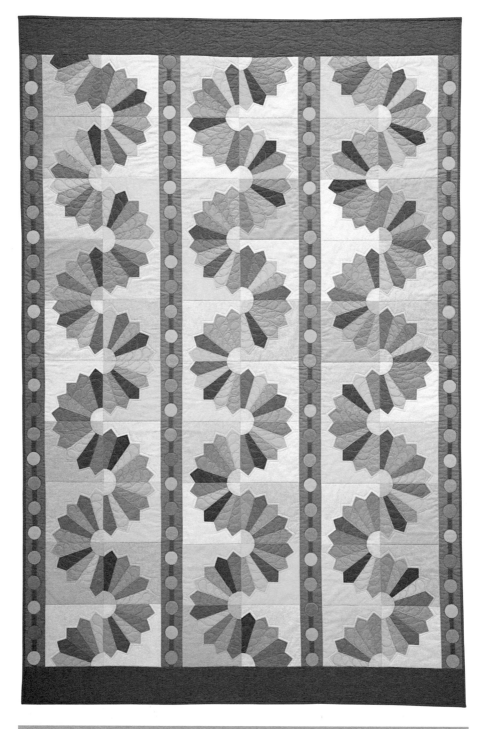

FINISHED BLOCKS: 8" × 8" • FINISHED QUILT: 60½" × 90"

Lollipop

Pieced by Amanda Murphy;
quilted by Deborah Norris

MATERIALS

SLINKY BLOCKS AND LOLLIPOP FABRIC: 33 fat quarters from 2 or 3 Kona fat quarter bundles (I used Poseidon, My Blue Heaven, and Greener Pastures.)

LOLLIPOP STICKS FABRIC: 1/3 yard Kona 357 Lapis

LOLLIPOP COLUMN BACKGROUND FABRIC: 1 1/8 yards Kona 1141 Fern

TOP AND BOTTOM BORDER FABRIC: 3/4 yard Kona 357 Lapis

BINDING FABRIC: 5/8 yard Kona 357 Lapis

BACKING FABRIC: 5 1/2 yards Kona 199 Cactus

PAPER-BACKED FUSIBLE WEB, 24" WIDE: 1 1/2 yards

PAPER-BACKED FUSIBLE TAPE, 1/4" WIDE: 1 package or 40 yards (I like Lite Steam-A-Seam 2.)

BATTING: 68" × 98" (I like Warm & Natural batting by the Warm Company.)

APPLIQUÉ THREAD: 12-, 28-, or 30-weight cotton thread (I use 28-weight Aurifil thread.)

INVISIBLE NYLON THREAD (I like YLI Wonder.)

DRESDEN PLATE OR 18° WEDGE RULER, such as Easy Dresden by Darlene Zimmerman or fast2cut Dresden Plate Template by C&T Publishing (see Supplies/Source List, page 143), *optional but highly recommended*

1/2" FUSIBLE BIAS TAPE MAKER, *optional but highly recommended* (I like Clover's.)

CUTTING
INSTRUCTIONS   WOF = width of fabric

FROM EACH OF THE 15 LIGHTEST FAT QUARTERS

- Cut 2 strips 8 1/2" × 18". Subcut into 4 squares 8 1/2" × 8 1/2".

- Cut 1 strip 2 1/2" × 18". Subcut into 4 squares 2 1/2" × 2 1/2".

FROM EACH OF THE REMAINING 18 FAT QUARTERS

- Cut 2 strips 6" × 20". Set aside excess fabric to use for the Lollipop circles. From the 6"-wide strips, cut 300 wedges, using the Dresden Plate Pattern (page 82) or the Easy Dresden ruler lined up on the 6" line. If you are using another 18° wedge ruler, place the ruler so the wide end of the wedge measures 2 7/8" and the narrow end measures 1". Use tape to mark the top and bottom edges of the fabric strip on your ruler.

FROM LOLLIPOP STICK FABRIC

- Cut 9 strips 1" × WOF. Piece into 4 rectangles 1" × 82".

FROM LOLLIPOP BACKGROUND FABRIC

- Cut 9 strips 4" × WOF. Piece into 4 rectangles 4" × 82".

FROM TOP AND BOTTOM BORDER FABRIC

- Cut 4 strips 5 1/4" × WOF. Piece into 2 rectangles 5 1/4" × 60 1/2".

FROM PAPER-BACKED FUSIBLE WEB

- Cut 60 squares 2 1/2" × 2 1/2". Set the remainder of the fusible web aside.

FROM BINDING FABRIC

- Cut 8 strips 2 1/4" × WOF.

Template Patterns

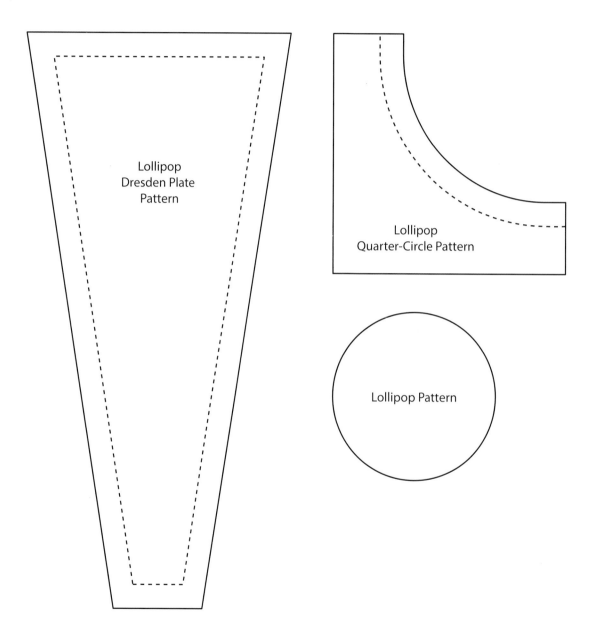

Lollipop
Dresden Plate
Pattern

Lollipop
Quarter-Circle Pattern

Lollipop Pattern

Slinky Block Assembly

Use a ¼" seam allowance unless noted otherwise.

1. Fold the Dresden Plate pieces in half lengthwise, right sides together, and sew across the wider end of the blade, using a ¼" seam allowance and backstitching at both ends of the seam. Clip the seam allowance of the folded corner to reduce bulk. Finger-press the seam open and turn right side out. Press. Repeat to make 300 Dresden Plate blades. **FIGURE A**

2. Sew the sides of 5 blades together to form a quarter of a Dresden Plate. Following the manufacturer's instructions, fuse short pieces of paper-backed fusible tape onto the outside edges of the wrong side of the plate. Remove the paper and arrange the entire plate onto the corner of a fat quarter square 8½" × 8½", aligning the raw edges. Fuse. Attach using an invisible hem stitch or narrow appliqué stitch with invisible nylon thread. Repeat to make 60 quarter–Dresden Plate blocks. **FIGURE B**

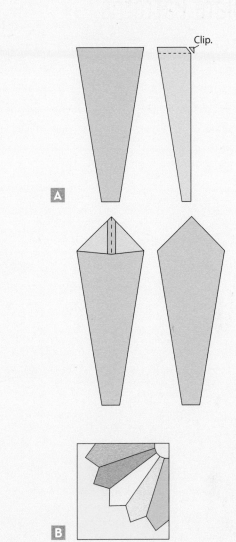

A

B

Clip.

3. Trace the Quarter-Circle Pattern (page 82) onto the smooth side of each of the 60 paper-backed fusible web 2½" × 2½" squares. Cut out excess fusible web from the inner part of the arc shape. Fuse a quarter-circle shape onto each of the 2½" × 2½" squares of light fat quarter fabric, aligning the straight edges of the fusible web with the straight edges of the fabric. Cut out the quarter-circles on the dashed line. **FIGURE C**

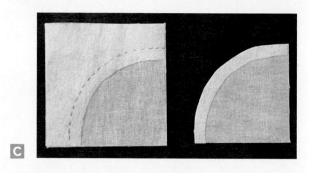

4. Remove the paper and fuse each quarter-circle to the center of a Dresden Plate block *with a matching background*, using the background fabric to align the corners of the quarter-circles. Cut the excess background fabric from behind each Dresden Plate. Refer to Fusible Appliqué (page 63) to machine appliqué the quarter-circles to secure them to the blocks, using a blanket or zigzag stitch and matching cotton thread. (You do not need stabilizer because the Dresden Plates will provide stability, nor do you need to knot the threads, as they will be buried in the seams.) **FIGURE D**

Lollipop Column Assembly

1. Refer to the product instructions to run the pieced Lollipop stick rectangles 1″ × 82 ″ through the fusible bias tape maker while applying fusible tape. If you don't have a fusible bias tape maker, fold the rectangles lengthwise so that the edges meet in the center, wrong sides together, and apply the fusible side of the paper-backed fusible web strips to the back (folded) side of your fabric strip. Following the manufacturer's instructions, fuse to the folded strip, and then remove the paper backing. **FIGURE E**

2. Fuse a Lollipop stick down the center of each pieced Lollipop background rectangle 4″ × 82″. Secure using an invisible hem stitch and trim the stick flush with the top and bottom of the column, if needed.

3. Trace the Lollipop Pattern (page 82) onto the smooth side of the paper-backed fusible web 100 times. Cut out extra fusible web from the center of each circle so the quilt top won't be stiff. Fuse the circles onto assorted extra fat quarter fabric. Cut out the circles on the drawn line.

4. Following the assembly diagram, arrange 25 circles evenly down each Lollipop column, centered on the Lollipop sticks. Fuse the circle in the middle of the column first and work your way toward the ends, placing 12 circles on either side of the center circle, 1½″ apart. Refer to Fusible Appliqué (page 63) to secure the circles to the column, using a blanket or zigzag stitch.

5. Trim the Lollipop columns to rectangles 3½″ × 80½″, centering the circle motifs.

Quilt Assembly

1. Following the assembly diagram, arrange the Dresden Plate blocks in 3 columns. Each column should be 2 blocks across and 10 blocks down. Join sets of 2 blocks into rows. Press the seams of the first row of each column to the right, the second to the left, and so on.

2. Join the rows to form 3 Slinky columns.

3. Following the assembly diagram, join the Slinky and Lollipop columns.

4. Join the top and bottom borders to the quilt top.

Assembly diagram

Finishing

1. Divide the backing fabric into 2 lengths. Cut 1 piece lengthwise to make 2 narrow panels. Join 1 narrow panel to each side of the wide panel. Press the seams open.

2. Layer the backing, batting, and quilt top. Quilt as desired.

3. See Binding (page 141) to make the binding and bind the quilt.

COLOR POSSIBILITIES

Field of Iris, True Blue, and Farmers Market

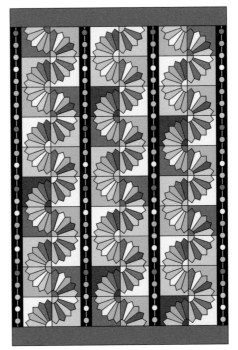

True Blue, Field of Iris, and Pretty Peonies

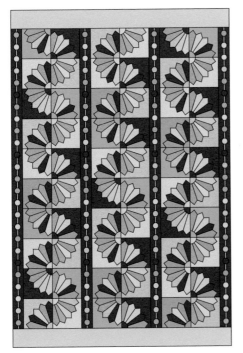

Sunset

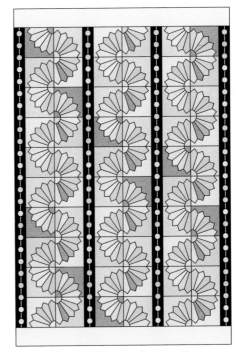

Grecian Waters and Burning Up

Iridescence

Make an easy, unique quilt using just one fat quarter bundle. Change the background fabric to create a unique look.

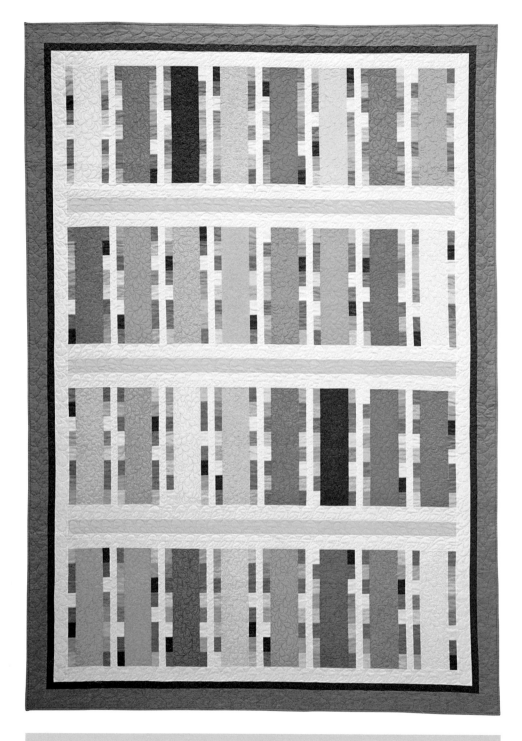

Iridescence—**Sunrise palette**

Pieced by Amanda Murphy;
quilted by Deborah Norris

MATERIALS

BLOCKS: 1 Kona Sunrise fat quarter bundle (or at least 16 fat quarters)

HORIZONTAL ACCENT BAR FABRIC: ½ yard Kona 21 Honey Dew or 145 Pear

BACKGROUND FABRIC: 2¼ yards Kona 1279 Pale Flesh

INNER BORDER FABRIC: ⅜ yard Kona 1049 Bright Pink

OUTER BORDER FABRIC: ⅞ yard Kona 192 Mango

BINDING FABRIC: ⅝ yard Kona 192 Mango

BACKING FABRIC: 6 yards Kona 1049 Bright Pink

BATTING: 75″ × 102″ (I like Warm & Natural batting by the Warm Company.)

CUTTING INSTRUCTIONS

WOF = width of fabric

FROM EACH OF 16 FAT QUARTERS
- Cut 2 strips 4½″ × 20″. Subcut into 2 rectangles 4½″ × 16½″.
- Cut 3 strips 2½″ × 20″.

FROM HORIZONTAL ACCENT BAR FABRIC
- Cut 5 strips 2½″ × WOF.

FROM BACKGROUND FABRIC
- Cut 14 strips 1½″ × WOF. Subcut into 28 rectangles 1½″ × 16½″.
- Cut 20 strips 2½″ × WOF.

FROM INNER BORDER FABRIC
- Cut 8 strips 1½″ × WOF.

FROM OUTER BORDER FABRIC
- Cut 8 strips 3¼″ × WOF.

FROM BINDING FABRIC
- Cut 9 strips 2¼″ × WOF.

Block Assembly

Use a ¼″ seam allowance unless noted otherwise.

1. Join 8 fat quarter strips 2½″ wide to make 1 strip set. Repeat to make a total of 6 strip sets. Cut a total of 64 units 1½″ wide from these sets. Press the seams open. **FIGURE A**

2. Join 1 of these units to each side of each fat quarter rectangle 4½″ × 16½″. **FIGURE B**

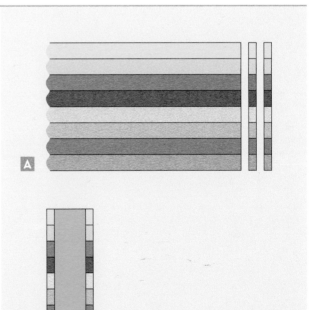

Quilt Assembly

1. Following the assembly diagram, join 8 blocks and 7 background rectangles 1½" × 16½". Repeat to make 4 rows.

2. Piece the background strips 2½" × WOF into 8 rectangles 2½" × 55½". Reserve the remaining strips for the inner border.

3. Join background rectangles 2½" × 55½" to the top and bottom of each row.

4. Piece the 6 horizontal accent bar strips 2½" × WOF into 3 rectangles 2½" × 55½".

5. Join the 4 block rows to the 3 horizontal accent bar rectangles to form the quilt top.

My quilt top at this point measured 55½" × 86½". Measure your quilt horizontally and vertically through the center and adjust the border measurements that follow if needed.

6. Piece the remaining background strips 2½" × WOF into 2 rectangles 2½" × 86½".

7. Join a background rectangle 2½" × 86½" onto each side of the quilt top.

8. Piece 2 inner border rectangles 1½" × 86½" and sew onto the sides of the quilt top. Piece 2 inner border rectangles 1½" × 61½" and sew onto the top and bottom of the quilt top.

9. Piece 2 outer border rectangles 3¼" × 88½" and sew onto the sides of the quilt top. Piece 2 outer border rectangles 3¼" × 67" and sew onto the top and bottom of the quilt top.

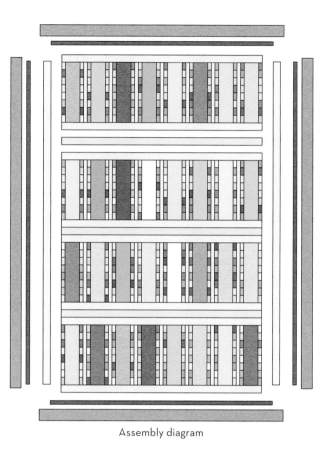

Assembly diagram

Finishing

1. Divide the backing fabric into 2 lengths. Cut 1 piece lengthwise to make 2 narrow panels. Join 1 narrow panel to each side of the wide panel. Press the seams open.

2. Layer the backing, batting, and quilt top. Baste. Quilt as desired.

3. See Binding (page 141) to make the binding and bind the quilt.

COLOR POSSIBILITIES

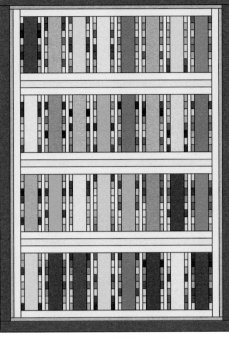

Sunset on 1275 Pale Mint

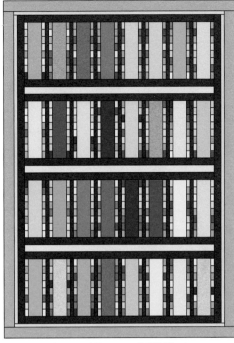

Grecian Waters on 1019 Black

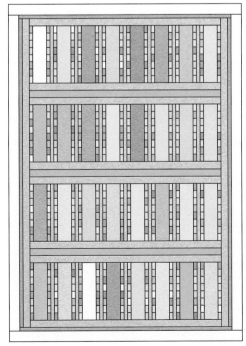

Pastel on 1225 Medium Pink

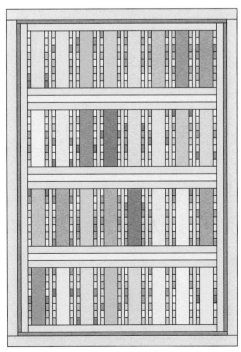

Pastel on 194 Lake

On Pointe

Setting squares on point creates movement. Traditional prairie points are given a new lease on life with a modern twist!

FINISHED QUILT: 46" × 60"

On Pointe—Sunset palette

Pieced by Amanda Murphy;
quilted by Deborah Norris

MATERIALS

BLOCKS: 1 Kona Sunset fat quarter bundle (or at least 16 fat quarters)

FRAME FABRIC: ¾ yard Kona 357 Lapis

HORIZONTAL BAND MAIN FABRIC: ⅝ yard Kona 318 Grapemist

HORIZONTAL BAND TRIANGLE FABRIC: ⅓ yard Kona 1387 White

BORDER FABRIC: ¾ yard Kona 1010 Baby Blue

BINDING FABRIC: ½ yard Kona 1010 Baby Blue

BACKING FABRIC: 4 yards Kona 318 Grapemist

BATTING: 54″ × 68″ (I like Warm & Natural batting by the Warm Company.)

CUTTING
INSTRUCTIONS   WOF = width of fabric

FROM EACH OF 16 FAT QUARTERS

- Cut 1 strip 5¼″ × 18″. Subcut into 3 squares 5¼″ × 5¼″. Cut each square diagonally twice into 4 quarter-square triangles.

- Cut 1 strip 5″ × 18″. Subcut into 2 squares 5″ × 5″.

- Cut 1 strip 3⅜″ × 18″. Subcut into 3 squares 3⅜″ × 3⅜″.

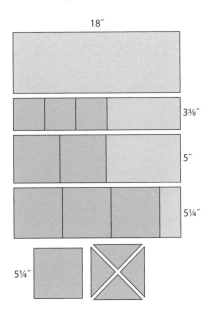

FROM FRAME FABRIC

- Cut 1 strip 12½″ × WOF. Subcut into 27 rectangles 1½″ × 12½″.

- Cut 8 strips 1½″ × WOF. Piece into 6 rectangles 1½″ × 41½″.

FROM HORIZONTAL BAND MAIN FABRIC

- Cut 3 strips 3½″ × WOF. Piece into 2 rectangles 3½″ × 41½″.

- Cut 5 strips 1⅞″ × WOF.

FROM HORIZONTAL BAND TRIANGLE FABRIC

- Cut 5 strips 1⅞″ × WOF.

FROM BORDER FABRIC

- Cut 3 strips 2¾″ × WOF.

- Cut 3 strips 4¼″ × WOF.

FROM BINDING FABRIC

- Cut 6 strips 2¼″ × WOF.

Framed Block Assembly

Use a ¼" seam allowance unless noted otherwise.

1. Join 2 quarter-square triangles to opposite sides of a square 3⅜" × 3⅜", aligning the straight edges, and press the seams toward the center square. Repeat to make 48 units. **FIGURE A**

2. Join 2 quarter-square triangles together along the short sides as shown, leaving seams unpressed. Repeat to make 48 units. **FIGURE B**

3. Join 2 rows of 2 units and 2 rows of 3 units as shown to form a block, pressing seams of 2-unit rows so they nest with seams of adjoining rows. Repeat to make a total of 24 blocks. **FIGURE C**

4. Trim the blocks to 4½" × 12½" if needed. Be sure to follow the diagram to keep the square and triangle points right at the seamline. The intersections where the seams meet are ¼" in from the edge of the fabric, as shown by the dashed line. *Note: The dashed line is the seamline and the solid line is the cutting line.* **FIGURE D**

5. Following the assembly diagram (page 100), join 8 blocks with 9 frame rectangles 1½" × 12½" to form a row. Repeat to make 3 rows.

6. Join frame rectangles 1½" × 41½" to the top and bottom of each row.

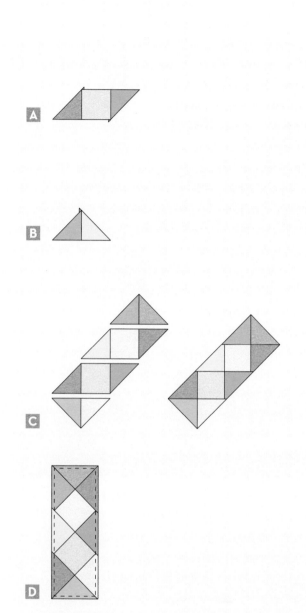

Horizontal Band Assembly

1. Join a horizontal band main fabric strip 1⅞″ × WOF to a horizontal band triangle fabric strip 1⅞″ × WOF and press the seams toward the main fabric. Repeat to make a total of 5 strip sets. Cut 88 units 1⅞″ wide from these strip sets. **FIGURE E**

2. Piece 4 sets of 22 units together, staggering the units as shown. **FIGURES F & G**

3. Trim these units to create a 1½″ × 41½″ rectangle, centering the triangles and making sure that the intersections where the seams meet are ¼″ in from the edge of the fabric as shown. *Note: The dashed line is the seamline and the solid line is the cutting line.* **FIGURE H**

4. Join pieced triangle strips to both the top and bottom of both horizontal band rectangles 3⅜″ × 41½″. **FIGURE I**

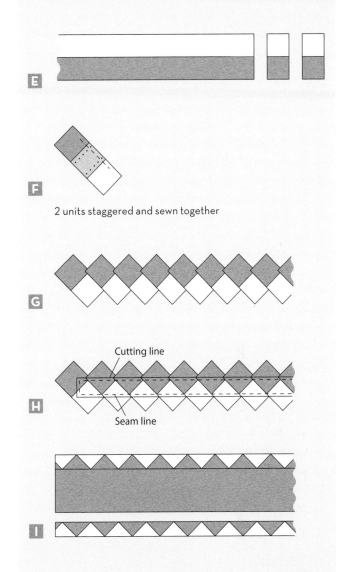

E

F

2 units staggered and sewn together

G

Cutting line

H

Seam line

I

Prairie Points

Fold all the 5″ × 5″ squares in half diagonally, wrong sides together, and press. Fold again in half to form quarter-square triangles. Press. Set aside. **FIGURE J**

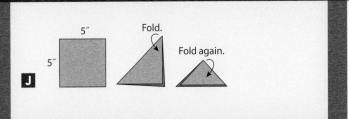

J

5″

5″

Fold.

Fold again.

Quilt Assembly

1. Following the assembly diagram (at right), arrange the 3 framed block rows with the 2 horizontal band rows. Sew the rows together.

2. *Measure your quilt horizontally and vertically through the center and adjust the border measurements that follow if needed.* Piece 2 rectangles 2¾" × 52½" from the 3 border strips 2¾" × WOF. Piece 2 rectangles 4¼" × 46½" from the 3 border strips 4¼" × WOF.

3. Join a border rectangle 2¾" × 52½" to each side of the quilt top.

4. Join border rectangles 4¼" × 46½" to the top and bottom of the quilt top.

5. Following the diagram, arrange 13 prairie points evenly across the top of your quilt, with the points pointing toward the quilt center, aligning the raw edges and allowing the prairie points to extend ¼" beyond each end of the quilt. Make sure all double-folded edges face the

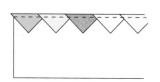

same direction! (There will be approximately a 1½" overlap on the raw edges of the points.) Pin and sew to the quilt using a ¼" seam allowance. Repeat this step to apply prairie points to the bottom edge of the quilt. You will have 6 extra prairie points.

Assembly diagram

Finishing

1. Divide the backing fabric into 2 lengths. Cut 1 piece lengthwise to make 2 narrow panels. Join 1 narrow panel to each side of the wide panel. Press the seams open.

2. Layer the backing, batting, and quilt top. Baste. Quilt as desired, but make sure that the quilting *does not come within* 1" of the quilt top or bottom and that the prairie points are held away from the quilt while quilting the border!

3. Trim the backing and batting to ½" beyond the seam that secures the prairie points. Trim the *batting only* down to the seamline. Turn the prairie points toward the

outside of the quilt—the seam allowances will be turned toward the inside. Press. Wrap the backing around the edge of the batting, under the quilt top and prairie points. Press and hand stitch closed.

4. See Binding (page 141) to make the binding. Turn under 1 of the narrow edges of the binding and, starting at the top of the quilt top where it meets the prairie points, sew the binding to the quilt, trimming and turning under the edge of the binding once you get to the bottom of the quilt. Wrap the binding around to the back and hand stitch to secure. Repeat on the remaining side.

COLOR POSSIBILITIES

True Blue and Field of Iris on 1243 Navy

Grecian Waters on 1373 Teal Blue

Bright on 1387 White

Grecian Waters and Sweet Peas on 1005 Aqua

Color Burst

Who says quilts have to be rectangular?
This circular design enlivens any decor.

Color Burst—Bright palette

Pieced by Amanda Murphy;
quilted by Deborah Norris

MATERIALS

INNER DIAMONDS: 7/8 yard Kona 1007 Ash

RADIATING DIAMONDS: 1 Kona Bright roll-up

SASHING: 2½ yards Kona 1387 White

OUTER DIAMONDS: 5/8 yard
Kona 1049 Hot Pink

BIAS BINDING FABRIC: 1 yard
Kona 1383 Violet

BACKING FABRIC: 4½ yards Kona 1007 Ash

BATTING: 78″ × 78″ (I like Warm & White
batting by the Warm Company.)

CUTTING
INSTRUCTIONS

WOF = width of fabric

FROM SASHING FABRIC

• Cut 32 strips 2½″ × WOF.

FROM INNER DIAMOND FABRIC

• Enlarge the Inner Diamond Pattern 200%
and cut out 8 inner diamond shapes.

FROM OUTER DIAMOND FABRIC

• Enlarge the Outer Triangle pattern 200% and
cut out 16 outer triangle shapes. *Note: Make
sure the grain of the fabric is parallel to 1
of the 2 long edges of the triangle.*

FROM BINDING FABRIC

• For binding, cut enough strips 2¼″ wide *on
the bias* to measure 285″ in length, or cut
1 square 27″ × 27″ to make continuous
bias binding (page 142). *Do not* try
to make this quilt using straight-
grain binding or it will be difficult
to miter the concave corners.

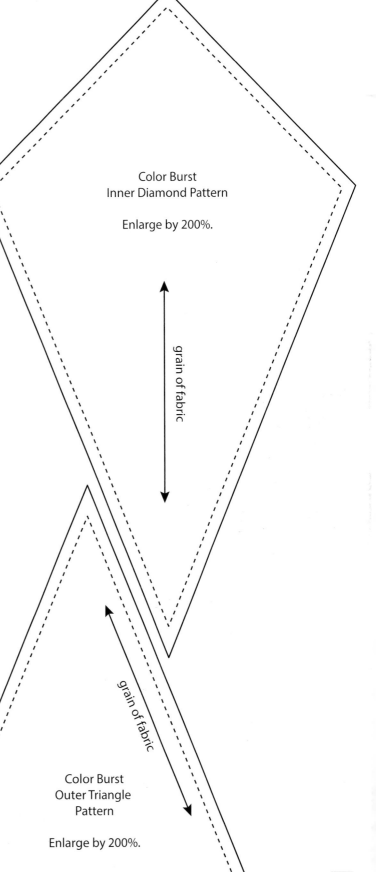

Color Burst
Inner Diamond Pattern

Enlarge by 200%.

grain of fabric

Color Burst
Outer Triangle
Pattern

Enlarge by 200%.

grain of fabric

Block Assembly

Now comes the really fun part ...

1. Take 1 roll-up and find 2 shades (a light and a dark) each of 16 colors, for a total of 32 roll-up strips. The colors don't have to match exactly, but should work well next to each other.

2. Join 1 strip of a dark fabric to 1 long side of an inner diamond. Press the seam toward the roll-up strip. Trim the strip flush with the block, aligning the template and your ruler with the edge of the inner diamond. *Note: Use the edges of the Inner Diamond Pattern to aid in trimming to keep the blocks the correct shape.* FIGURE A

3. Join the rest of the strip from Step 2 to the other long side of the inner diamond. Press the seam toward the roll-up strip. Trim the strip flush with the block using the Inner Diamond Pattern. FIGURE B

4. Join 1 strip of another of the dark fabrics to a short side of the inner diamond. Press the seam toward the roll-up strip. Trim the strip flush with the block using the Inner Diamond Pattern. FIGURE C

5. Join the rest of the strip from Step 4 to the other short side of the inner diamond. Press the seam toward the roll-up strip. Trim the strip flush with the block using the Inner Diamond Pattern. FIGURE D

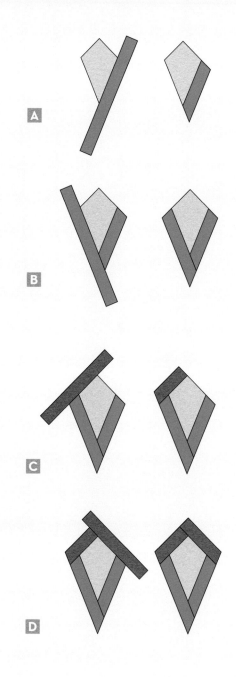

6. Join 1 strip of the lighter shade of the fabric you joined in Step 2 to the long side of this diamond block. Press the seam toward the roll-up strip. Trim the strip flush with the block using the Inner Diamond Pattern. **FIGURE E**

7. Join the rest of the strip from Step 6 to the other long side of the inner diamond. (*Note:* Make sure to align the top of this strip with the top of the diamond as shown, or you won't have enough fabric to cover the bottom point of the diamond!) Press the seam toward the roll-up strip. Trim the strip flush with the block using the Inner Diamond Pattern. **FIGURE F**

8. Join 1 strip of the lighter shade of the fabric you joined in Step 4 to a short side of this diamond block. Press the seam toward the roll-up strip. Trim the strip flush with the block using the Inner Diamond Pattern. **FIGURE G**

9. Join the rest of the remaining strip from Step 8 to the other short side of the inner diamond. Press the seam toward the roll-up strip. Trim the strip flush with the block using the Inner Diamond Pattern. **FIGURE H**

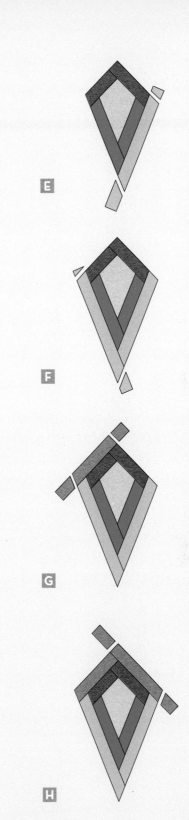

E

F

G

H

10. In the same manner, join 1 sashing strip to a long side of the diamond block. Press the seam toward the roll-up strip. Trim the strip flush with the block using the Inner Diamond Pattern. *If you are using a light sashing color, be sure to press the seams open in Steps 10–13.*

11. Join 1 sashing strip to the other long side of the diamond block. Press the seam toward the center of the block. Trim the strip flush with the block using the Inner Diamond Pattern.

12. Join 1 sashing strip to a short side of the diamond block. Press the seam toward the center of the block. Trim the strip flush with the block using the Inner Diamond Pattern.

13. Join 1 sashing strip to the other short side of the diamond block. Press the seam toward the center of the block. Trim the strip flush with the block using the Inner Diamond Template.

14. Attach 2 outer triangles to the diamond block, making sure that the straight grain of the triangles lie on what will become the outer edge of the quilt, as shown. **FIGURE I**

15. Repeat Steps 2–14 to make a total of 8 diamond blocks.

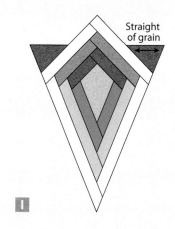
Straight of grain

1

Quilt Assembly

1. Following the assembly diagram, join 2 sets of 4 diamond blocks together, stopping and backstitiching ¼″ from the edges where all the seams meet in the center and leaving the last ¼″ open. Make sure the outer diamond seams align, and press all the seams in the same direction. Make sure the seams where the outer triangles are joined to the background strips meet, as this is much more noticeable than where the seams meet in the center of the quilt top.

2. Join sets of blocks, swirling the center seam allowance where all the seams meet. To do this, turn the quilt top wrong side up and stroke the seams in a uniform direction, either clockwise or counterclockwise, so that they lie flat. Press from the back of the quilt top and then press from the front of the quilt top.

3. If the quilt doesn't lie flat at this point, you might have to take in some of the seams between the blocks to compensate for any extra fabric at the quilt's edge. Do this by resewing a seam with a larger seam allowance that gradually tapers to the ¼″ seam allowance as you sew toward the center of the quilt top.

Assembly diagram

Finishing

1. Divide the backing fabric into 2 lengths. Join along the length. Press the seams open.

2. Layer the backing, batting, and quilt top. Baste. Quilt as desired.

3. Join the 2¼" *bias* binding strips into 1 continuous piece for binding. Starting on a straight side, sew the binding to the quilt. Miter the first exterior corner. Turn the quilt top so you are headed to an interior corner.

4. When you get to the first interior corner, stop with the needle down in the seam. Stretch the quilt so that the raw edge of the quilt is lying as straight as you can get it. This means the binding will also lie straight at the pivot point, but the quilt itself will be a little bunched up under the needle. Lower the presser foot and continue to sew about ½" more along the new side of the quilt. Release the quilt top and sew to the next corner.

5. Apply the rest of the binding in this manner.

6. Once you have applied the binding, clip the inside corner seam allowances of the *binding only*. This is very important. Don't clip the quilt sandwich!

7. Fold the binding over to the back and hand stitch to secure. I like to put a tiny extra stitch at each of the interior corners through all the layers of the fabric as I bind the quilt.

Aqua and green yardage on 1387 White

Sunrise on 1387 White

Green and blue yardage on 1019 Black

Pastel on 1214 Magenta

Confetti

Let the colors of your favorite fat quarter bundle shine in this lap-sized project. Straight-line quilting emphasizes the triangular blocks.

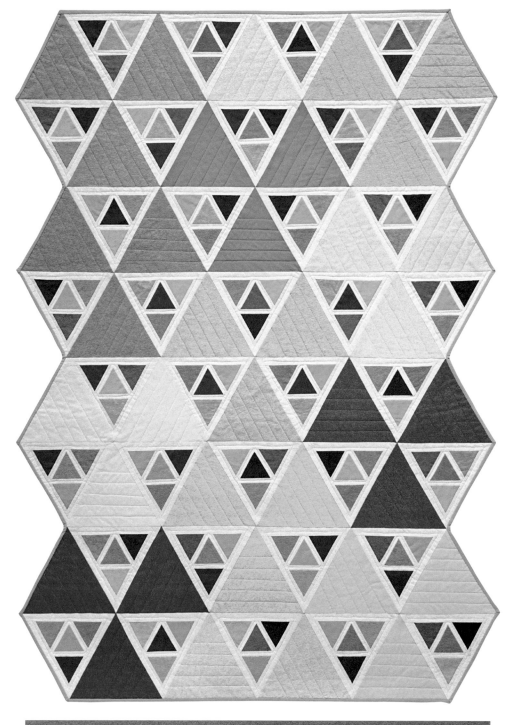

FINISHED BLOCKS: 8" triangles • FINISHED QUILT: 46" × 64"

Confetti—**Sunrise palette**

Pieced by Amanda Murphy;
quilted by Deborah Norris

MATERIALS

BLOCKS: 1 Kona Sunrise fat quarter bundle (or at least 21 fat quarters)

SASHING: 1¾ yards Kona 1216 Maize

BIAS BINDING FABRIC: 1 yard Kona 144 Sour Apple or 1370 Tangerine

BACKING FABRIC: 4½ yards Kona 192 Mango

BATTING: 54″ × 72″ (I like Warm & Natural batting by the Warm Company.)

60° BLUNT-TIP TRIANGLE RULER: 8″ (I like one made by Creative Grids.)

CUTTING
INSTRUCTIONS WOF = width of fabric

FROM EACH OF 13 FAT QUARTERS

• Cut 2 strips 8½″ × 18″.* Subcut into 3 triangles using the blunt-tip triangle ruler.

*If you don't have a *blunt-tip triangle ruler,* cut the strip 8¾″ wide. Use a rectangular ruler with a 60° mark to cut 3 equilateral triangles by rotating the ruler so the 60° mark is alternately aligned with the top and the bottom of the strip. You can also use a 60° triangle ruler without a blunt tip to cut 8″ finished triangles from the 8¾″-wide strips.

FROM EACH OF 8 FAT QUARTERS

• Cut 3 strips 3″ × 18″.* Subcut into 18 triangles using the blunt-tip triangle ruler.

*If you don't have a blunt-tip triangle ruler, cut the strips 3¼″ wide. Use a rectangular ruler with a 60° mark to cut 18 equilateral triangles by rotating the ruler so the 60° mark is alternately aligned with the top and the bottom of the strip. You can also use a 60° triangle ruler without a blunt tip to cut 3″ finished triangles from the 3¼″-wide strips.

FROM SASHING FABRIC

• Cut 17 strips 1″ × WOF.

• Cut 24 strips 1⅜″ × WOF.

FROM BIAS BINDING FABRIC

• For binding, cut enough strips 2¼″ wide on *the bias* to yield at least 250″ in length, or cut 1 square 25″ × 25″ to make continuous bias binding (page 142). *Do not try to make this quilt using straight-grain binding or it will be difficult to miter the inner corners.*

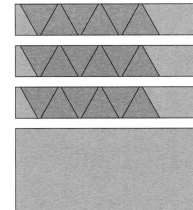

18″   18″

Little Triangle Block Assembly

1. Chain piece 1 side of each of 36 little triangles to 1″-wide sashing strips, making sure to leave at least 1¼″ of the strip unstitched between each triangle and the next. **FIGURE A**

2. Use your ruler to trim off the sashing strips flush with the triangles. **FIGURE B**

3. Chain piece another side of each of the 36 little triangles to 1″-wide sashing strips, making sure to leave at least 1¼″ of the strip unstitched between each triangle and the next. Use your ruler to trim off the sashing strips flush with the triangles. **FIGURE C**

4. Chain piece the third side of each of the 36 little triangles to 1″-wide sashing strips, making sure to leave at least 1¼″ of the strip unstitched between the triangles. Use your ruler to trim off the sashing strips flush with the triangles. **FIGURE D**

5. Trim the corners of these units using the Triangle Trimming Pattern. **FIGURE E**

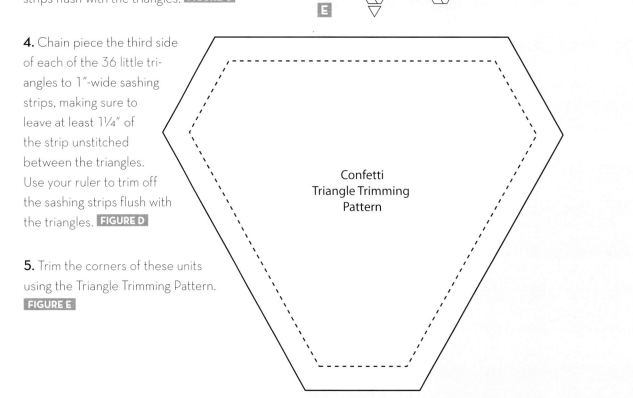

Confetti Triangle Trimming Pattern

6. Join a little triangle to each of the 3 sides of this unit. **FIGURE F**

7. In the same manner as Step 1, chain piece 1 side of each of the little triangle blocks to a 1⅜"-wide sashing strip, making sure to leave at least 2" of the strip unstitched between each triangle block and the next. Use your ruler to trim off the sashing strips flush with the raw edges. Repeat to apply sashing to the second and third sides of each little triangle block. **FIGURE G**

8. If necessary, trim all the pieced blocks down to 8½" triangles (measuring the height through the triangle, not along a side) using the triangle ruler or using the 60° line on a regular ruler. Each side should measure 10⅛".

Quilt Assembly

1. Following the assembly diagram, lay out the little triangle blocks and the big triangles to form the quilt top. (Note that the big triangles are arranged so 3 of the same color share a point.)

2. Join 5 large triangles with 4 little triangle blocks to form the first row. Repeat to make the third, fifth, and seventh rows.

3. Join 4 large triangles with 5 little triangle blocks to form the second row. Repeat to make the fourth, sixth, and eighth rows.

4. Join the rows.

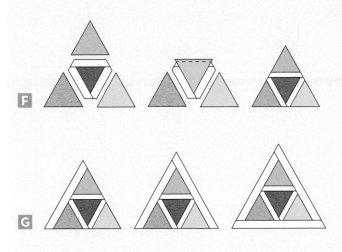

Assembly diagram

Finishing

1. Divide the backing fabric into 2 equal lengths. Join. Press the seams open.

2. Layer the backing, batting, and quilt top. Baste. Quilt as desired.

3. Join the 2¼"-wide *bias* binding strips into 1 continuous piece for binding. Starting on the top of the quilt, sew the binding to the quilt. Miter the first 2 exterior corners. Turn the quilt top so you are headed to an interior corner.

4. When you get to the first interior corner, stop with the needle down in the seam. Stretch the quilt top so that the raw edge of the quilt top is lying as straight as you can get it. This means the binding will also lie straight at the pivot point, but the quilt top itself will be a little bunched up under the needle. Lower the presser foot and continue to sew about ½" more along the new side of the quilt. Release the quilt top and sew to the next corner.

5. Apply the rest of the binding in this manner.

6. Once you have applied the binding, clip the inside corner seam allowances of the *binding only*. This is very important. Don't clip the quilt sandwich!

7. Fold the binding over to the back and hand stitch to secure. I like to put a tiny extra stitch at each of the interior corners through all the layers of fabric as I bind the quilt.

COLOR POSSIBILITIES

True Blue and Farmer's Market on 357 Lapis

Bright on 1005 Aqua

True Blue and Grecian Waters on 1019 Black

True Blue and Burning Up on 1005 Aqua

Spring Blooms

Contrast the warm Sunrise palette with cool Kona 1005 Aqua for a fresh look. Kona Quilter's Linen in the background adds textural interest.

FINISHED QUILT: 50" × 66"

Spring Blooms—Sunrise palette

Pieced by Amanda Murphy;
quilted by Deborah Norris

MATERIALS

FLOWER FABRICS: 1 Sunrise Kona roll-up (or at least 24 strips 2½" wide or scraps)

FLOWER GROUND FABRIC: 2½ yards Kona 1514 Robin Egg

BACKGROUND FABRIC: 1⅔ yards Kona Quilter's Linen 64 Azure (*Note: This quilt requires a 42" usable width of fabric so you can cut a rectangle 41" × 57". If you are unable to cut this width from your fabric, adjust the yardage needed accordingly.*)

INNER BORDER: ⅓ yard Kona 1370 Tangerine

OUTER BORDER: ⅞ yard Kona 1378 White

BINDING FABRIC: ⅝ yard Kona Quilter's Linen 64 Azure

BACKING FABRIC: 4½ yards Kona 139 Lagoon

STABILIZER, 20" WIDE: 2¾ yards (I like Sulky Tear-Easy.)

PAPER-BACKED FUSIBLE WEB, 12" WIDE: 1¾ yards (I like Lite Steam-a-Seam.)

SPRAY ADHESIVE (I like 505 Temporary Adhesive Spray.)

BATTING: 58" × 74" (I like Warm & Natural batting by the Warm Company.)

AN ASSORTMENT OF THREAD, including a color that matches the flower ground fabric (I like 28-weight Aurifil or 20-weight Sulky cotton threads.)

CUTTING
INSTRUCTIONS   WOF = width of fabric

FROM FLOWER GROUND FABRIC

• Cut 9 strips 8½" × WOF. Subcut into 24 squares 8½" × 8½" and 20 rectangles 8½" × 4½".

• Cut 1 strip 4½" × WOF. Subcut into 4 squares 4½" × 4½".

FROM BACKGROUND FABRIC

• Cut 1 rectangle 41" × 57". (If your fabric is not wide enough, piece to the required size.)

FROM INNER BORDER FABRIC

• Cut 6 strips 1½" × WOF.

FROM OUTER BORDER FABRIC

• Cut 6 strips 4¼" × WOF.

FROM BINDING FABRIC

• Cut 7 strips 2¼" × WOF.

Block Assembly

Use a ¼″ seam allowance unless noted otherwise.

1. Enlarge the Full Block Pattern, Half Block Pattern, and Quarter Block Pattern 200%.

2. Trace the Bloom Petal Pattern onto the smooth side of paper-backed fusible web 192 times. Trace the Bloom Center Pattern 24 times. Cut out excess fusible web from inside the shapes, leaving at least a ¼″ margin all around, so the finished quilt will not be stiff.

3. Following the manufacturer's instructions, fuse 8 Bloom Petals and 1 Bloom Center to each of the 24 roll-up strips. Cut out the shapes.

4. Fold each flower ground square 8½″ × 8½″ vertically, horizontally, and diagonally in both directions, pressing lightly each time.

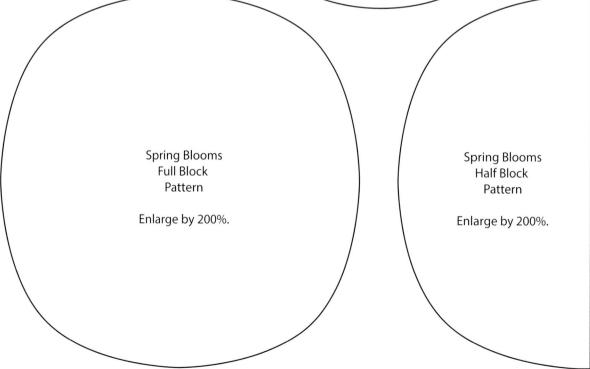

Spring Blooms
Quarter Block
Pattern

Enlarge by 200%.

Bloom
Center
Pattern

Spring Blooms
Bloom Petal Pattern

Spring Blooms
Full Block
Pattern

Enlarge by 200%.

Spring Blooms
Half Block
Pattern

Enlarge by 200%.

5. Remove the paper from the back of 4 petals of 1 color, 4 petals of another color, and 1 center of a third color and fuse to a flower ground square 8½″ × 8½″, using the fold lines as guides. **FIGURE A**

6. Refer to Fusible Appliqué (page 63) to appliqué the blooms, backing with tear-away stabilizer and using a blanket stitch with thick, contrasting threads. Bury and knot the threads.

7. Center and trace the enlarged Full Block Pattern over each appliquéd bloom block. Cut out on the drawn line. **FIGURE B**

8. Trace the enlarged Half Block Pattern onto each bloom ground rectangle 4½″ × 8½″. Cut out on the drawn line.

9. Trace the enlarged Quarter Block Pattern onto each bloom ground square 4½″ × 4½″. Cut out on the drawn line.

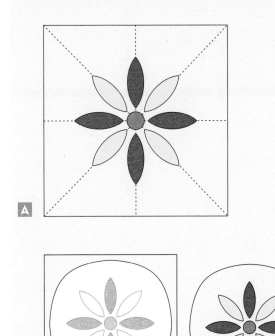

Quilt Assembly

1. Fold the background rectangle 41″ × 57″ in half vertically and horizontally. Press.

2. Mark a chalk line every 8″ from these lines. (There will be 4½″ of excess fabric beyond the outermost chalk lines.)

3. Spray the back of 4 appliquéd bloom blocks with adhesive spray. Center them in the 4 top squares defined by the chalk lines. Back with tear-away stabilizer behind the background fabric and appliqué using a blanket stitch in matching thread. Continue adding blocks to each row in this manner, working down the quilt.

4. Trim the quilt top to 40½" × 56½". You will trim about ¼" off each edge. The cutting line should be about 4¼" away from the outer chalk lines.

5. Spray the back of the quarter and half ground shapes with adhesive spray. Following the assembly diagram, apply the shapes to the outer rectangle and square areas, aligning the raw edges. Back with tear-away stabilizer and appliqué using a blanket stitch in matching thread. Remove excess stabilizer from the entire quilt top

6. *Measure your quilt horizontally and vertically through the center and adjust the border measurements that follow if needed.* Piece 2 rectangles 1½" × 42½" and 2 rectangles 1½" × 56½" from the inner border strips 1½" × WOF.

7. Piece 2 rectangles 4¼" × 50" and 2 rectangles 4¼" × 58½" from the outer border strips 4¼" × WOF.

8. Join the side inner borders to the quilt top.

9. Join the top and bottom inner borders to the quilt top.

10. Join the side outer borders to the quilt top.

11. Join the top and bottom outer borders to the quilt top.

Assembly diagram

Finishing

1. Divide the backing fabric into 2 lengths. Cut 1 piece lengthwise to make 2 narrow panels. Join 1 narrow panel to each side of the wide panel. Press the seams open.

2. Layer the backing, batting, and quilt top. Baste. Quilt as desired.

3. See Binding (page 141) to make the binding and bind the quilt.

COLOR POSSIBILITIES

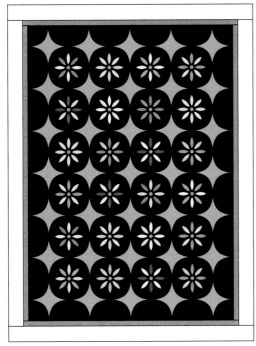

Sunrise on 1019 Black and 1282 Peacock

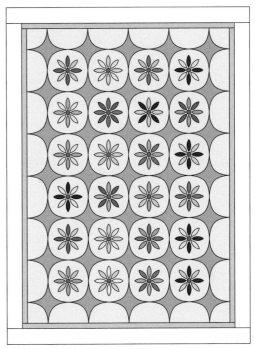

Blues and greens on 21 Honeydew and 1061 Candy Green

Purples and aquas on 1173 Ice Frappe and 1189 Lavender

Pinks and oranges on 1291 Pink and 192 Mango

Circus

Playful pennant shapes mimic the flags on a circus tent. Yo-yo accents add a whimsical touch.

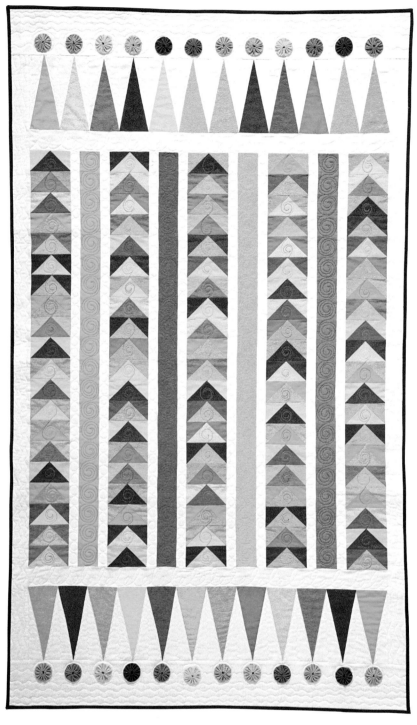

FINISHED QUILT: 40" × 66"

Circus—Sunrise palette

Pieced by Amanda Murphy;
quilted by Deborah Norris

MATERIALS

BLOCK FABRICS: 1 Kona Sunrise fat quarter bundle (or at least 13 fat quarters)

VERTICAL ACCENT BAR FABRICS: ⅛ yard* each of Kona 1089 Corn Yellow, 1265 Orange, 1049 Bright Pink, and 144 Sour Apple

BACKGROUND FABRIC: 1½* yards Kona 1387 White

BINDING FABRIC: ½ yard Kona 1295 Pomegranate

BACKING FABRIC: 2¾ yards Kona 199 Cactus

BATTING: 48″ × 74″ (I like Warm & White batting by the Warm Company.)

YO-YO MAKER for yo-yos finishing about 1½″ (I like Clover brand.)

* Requires minimum 41″ usable width of fabric, or additional yardage to piece.

CUTTING
INSTRUCTIONS `WOF = width of fabric`

FROM EACH OF 13 FAT QUARTERS OF FABRIC

- Cut 2 strips 2⅞″ × 18″. Subcut into 8 squares 2⅞″ × 2⅞″.

- Cut 1 strip 5¼″ × 18″. Subcut into 2 squares 5¼″ × 5¼″.

- Cut 1 strip 7½″ × 18″. Cut 2 Triangle A units using the pattern (page 132).

- Set the remainder of the fabric aside for yo-yos.

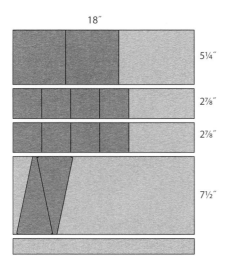

FROM VERTICAL ACCENT BAR FABRICS

- Cut (or piece, if necessary, depending on the width of the fabric) 1 rectangle 2½″ × 40½″ from each color of fabric.

FROM BACKGROUND FABRIC

- Cut 8 strips 1½″ × WOF. Subcut (or piece, if needed) into 8 rectangles 1½″ × 40½″.

- Cut 3 strips 2¼″ × WOF. Piece and subcut into 2 rectangles 2¼″ × 58½″.

- Cut 2 strips 2½″ × WOF. Subcut into 2 rectangles 2½″ × 36½″.

- Cut 2 strips 4¼″ × WOF. Subcut into 2 rectangles 4¼″ × 40″.

- Cut 2 strips 7½″ × WOF. Subcut into 22 Triangle A units and 4 Triangle B units as shown using the patterns (page 132).

FROM BINDING FABRIC

- Cut 6 strips 2¼″ × WOF.

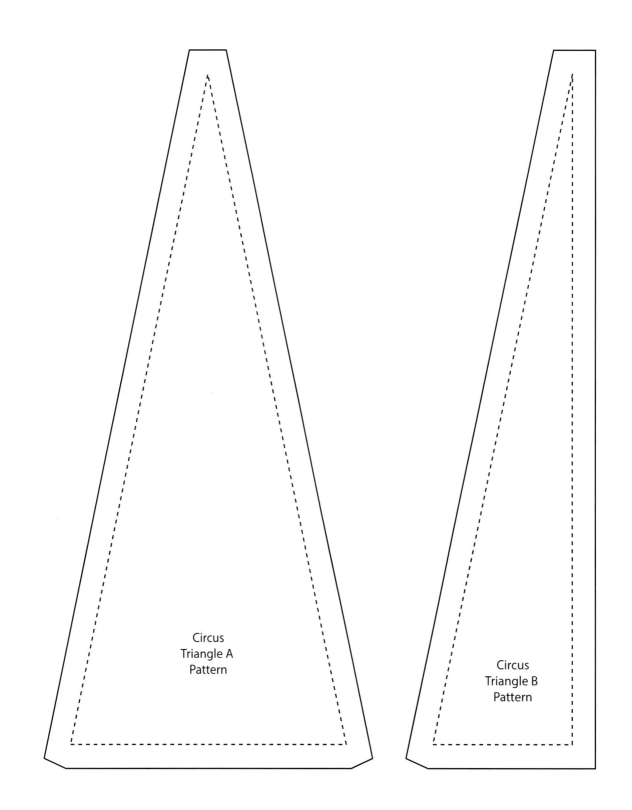

Circus
Triangle A
Pattern

Circus
Triangle B
Pattern

Tall Triangle Row Assembly

Use a ¼″ seam allowance unless noted otherwise.

Join 12 Triangle A units together with 11 background Triangle A units and 2 background Triangle B units to form a triangle row. Press the seams open. Repeat to make a second row.
FIGURE A

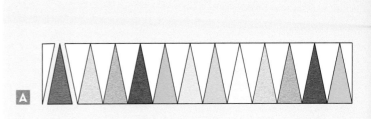

Vertical Stripe Assembly

Join a background rectangle 1½″ × 40½″ to each long side of each vertical accent bar rectangle 2½″ × 40½″. Make 4.

Flying Geese Block Assembly

1. Refer to Easy Flying Geese (page 137), to make 4 Flying Geese units, using 1 square 5¼″ × 5¼″ and 4 contrasting squares 2⅞″ × 2⅞″ of the same fabric. Press the seams open. Repeat the process with all the remaining squares 5¼″ × 5¼″ and 2⅞″ × 2⅞″ to make 100 Flying Geese.

2. Following the assembly diagram (page 135), join the Flying Geese into 4 columns of 20 geese each.

Quilt Assembly

1. Following the assembly diagram, join the Flying Geese columns together with vertical accent bar columns to form the quilt top center.

2. Join the background rectangles 2½″ × 36½″ to the top and bottom of the quilt top center.

3. Join the tall triangle rows to the top and bottom of the quilt top center.

4. Join a background rectangle 2¼″ × 58½″ to each side of the quilt top.

5. Join background rectangles 4¼″ × 40″ to the top and bottom of the quilt top.

6. Make 24 yo-yos using a strong thread, such as buttonhole thread. (If you don't have a yo-yo maker, cut out 24 circles 4″ in diameter. Take a large running stitch around the edge, turning under the fabric ¼″ as you go. Pull tight, knot, and bury the threads.)

7. Attach a yo-yo at the tip of each tall triangle as shown at right. Thread a needle with thread that matches the color of the yo-yo. Knot the end of the thread, leaving at least 3″ of thread beyond the knot. Come up through the *wrong side* of the quilt top about 1″ from the tip of the tall triangle. Come up through the center of the yo-yo and go back down through both the center of the yo-yo and the quilt top. Make a knot with the tail end of the thread, but don't cut the thread. **FIGURE B**

8. Travel between the layers to a point at the yo-yo's edge. Come up through the edge of the yo-yo. **FIGURE C**

9. Make a tiny backstitch and go back down through all the layers. Travel about ¼″ along the yo-yo's edge and come back up. Make a tiny backstitch. Proceed to sew all around the yo-yo's edge, making tiny backstitches about ¼″ apart. **FIGURE D**

10. When you arrive back at your starting point, travel back to the tail end of your thread through both fabric layers and make another knot. **FIGURE E**

Trim the threads to about ½″. Repeat to attach a yo-yo to each tall triangle point. (You can also attach the yo-yos using tacking stitches on your sewing machine if you prefer.)

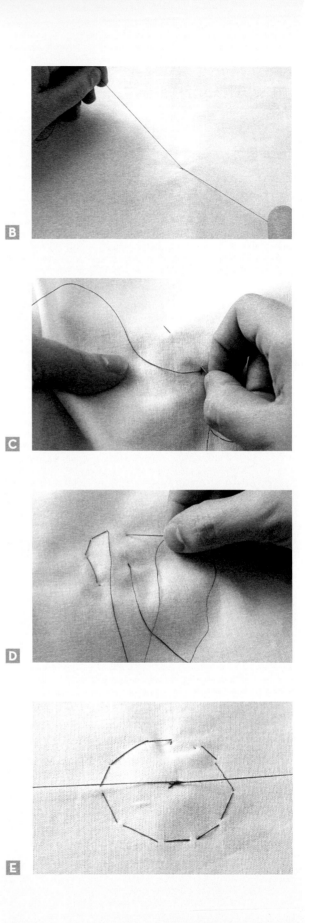

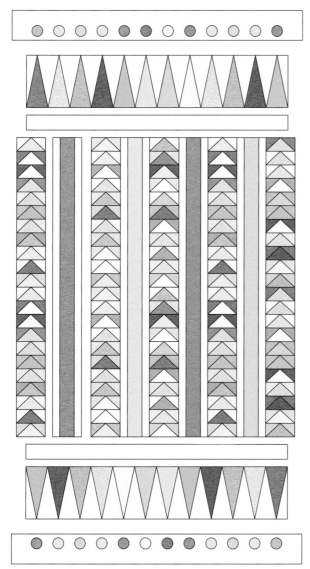

Assembly diagram

Finishing

1. Cut 2 strips 9″ × WOF from the backing fabric. Join the short sides together.

2. Cut the remaining fabric lengthwise to make 2 narrow panels. Insert the pieced unit between the panels. Press the seams open.

3. Layer the backing, batting, and quilt top. Baste. Quilt as desired.

4. See Binding (page 141) to make the binding and bind the quilt.

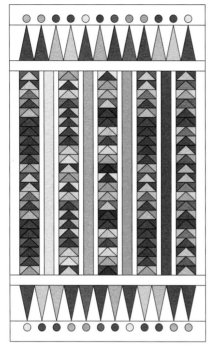

Burning Up, Pretty Peonies, and Fields of Iris on 1387 White

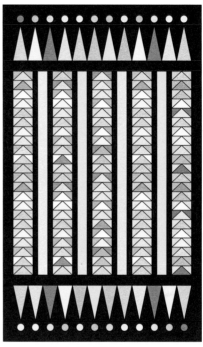

Pastel on 80 Mulberry

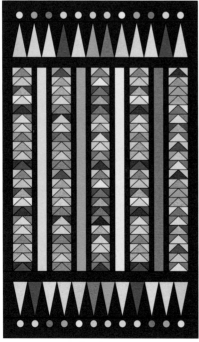

Sunset on 1232 Midnight

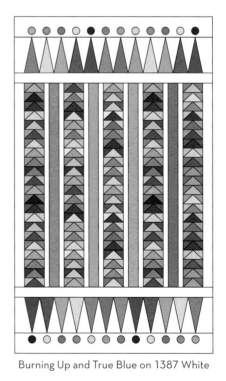

Burning Up and True Blue on 1387 White

Easy Flying Geese

There are many great Flying Geese templates on the market today to help you make Flying Geese quickly and accurately. If you are using a template, adjust these cutting directions accordingly. If you prefer not to use a template, here is a simple method to make 4 Flying Geese (2″ × 4″ finished) at a time.

1. Cut 1 square 5¼″ × 5¼″ for the geese and 4 matching squares 2⅞″ × 2⅞″ for the sky. Draw a diagonal line from corner to corner on the wrong side of all the 2⅞″ × 2⅞″ squares. Align 2 fabric squares 2⅞″ × 2⅞″ on opposite corners of the background square 5¼″ × 5¼″, right sides together, as shown. Stitch a scant ¼″ away from both sides of the drawn diagonal line. **FIGURE A**

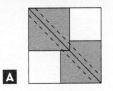

A

2. Cut along the drawn line. **FIGURE B**

B

Open out the triangles. Press the seams open or toward the geese, as specified in the project's directions. **FIGURE C**

C

3. Align another square 2⅞″ × 2⅞″ on the remaining unsewn corners of these 2 units, right sides together. Sew ¼″ away from both sides of the drawn lines. **FIGURE D**

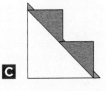

4. Cut along the drawn lines. Open out the triangles and press. Trim the units to 2½″ × 4½″ if needed. **FIGURE E**

D

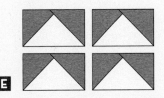

E

Quilting Solids

Some thoughts from Deborah Norris of Deborah's Quilting:

My work as a professional longarm quilter varies with each customer's quilt, but working with Amanda Murphy is truly exciting since she designs her own quilt patterns. My first thought when I see them is often, "Wow! What will I do with this design?" It is challenging and fun to interpret Amanda's designs and add my element of quilting to her tops.

The projects for this book added the challenge and fun of quilting on solids, since prints in fabrics often help stir my creative juices. The Kona cottons are beautiful! And I often felt as if I had a "clean slate" to work on with the solids (although Amanda's piecing and appliqué were also an influence). You'll notice that I often matched the thread to the color of the fabrics, which somehow seemed "safer," but at times I really had fun using variegated thread. It often surprised me when I finished a quilt and stood back to view it.

So be daring, be bold in your quilting thread colors, and, above all, have fun using the Kona cottons in Amanda's latest designs.

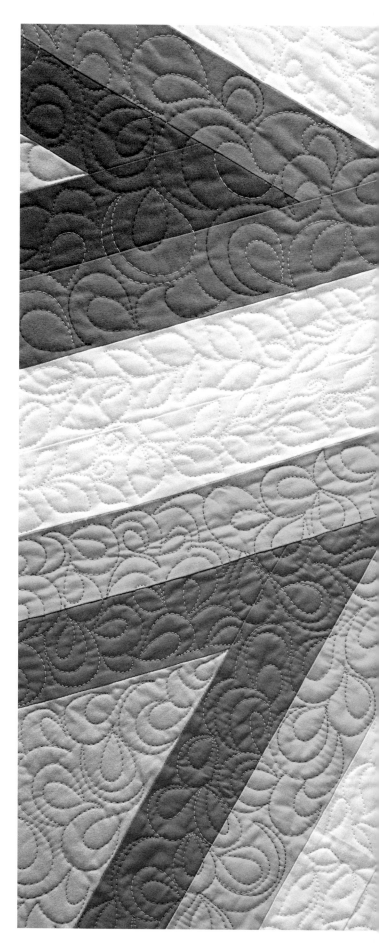

Quiltmaking Basics

- Seam allowances for all the projects in this book are ¼", unless otherwise noted.

- WOF stands for "width of fabric."

- All required yardage is based on a fabric width of 40" to account for the trimming of selvages and shrinkage if the fabric is prewashed, unless otherwise noted.

- A fat quarter refers to a 1-yard piece of fabric that has been cut in half once on its length and again on its width, to yield a piece approximately 18" × 21".

Borders

When you have finished the quilt top, measure it through the center vertically. This will be the length to cut the side borders. Piece the strips together to achieve the needed lengths. Place pins at the centers of all 4 sides of the quilt top, as well as in the center of each side border strip. Pin the side borders to the quilt top first, matching the center pins. Sew the borders to the quilt top and press toward the border.

Measure horizontally across the center of the quilt top, including the side borders. This will be the length to cut the top and bottom borders. Repeat the pinning, sewing, and pressing.

Backing

Plan on making the backing a minimum of 8" longer and wider than the quilt top. Piece, if necessary.

Batting

These quilts feature Warm & Natural or Warm & White cotton batting. Cut the batting approximately 8" longer and wider than your quilt top.

Layering

Spread the backing wrong side up on a flat surface and tape the edges down with masking tape. (If you are working on carpet you can use T-pins to secure the backing to the carpet.) Center the batting on top, smoothing out any folds. Place the quilt top right side up on top of the batting and backing, making sure it is centered.

Basting

Basting keeps the quilt "sandwich" layers from shifting while you are quilting.

If you plan to machine quilt, pin baste the quilt layers together with safety pins placed about 3"–4" apart. For hand quilting, thread baste.

Quilting

Quilting, whether by hand or machine, enhances the pieced or appliquéd design of the quilt. You may choose to quilt in-the-ditch, echo the pieced or appliqué motifs, use patterns from quilting design books and stencils, or do your own free-motion quilting. Remember to check the batting manufacturer's recommendations for how close the quilting lines must be.

Binding

Trim excess batting and backing from the quilt even with the edges of the quilt top.

If you want a ¼" finished binding, cut the binding strips 2¼" wide and piece them together with diagonal seams to make a continuous binding strip. Trim the seam allowance to ¼". Press the seams open. **FIGURES A&B**

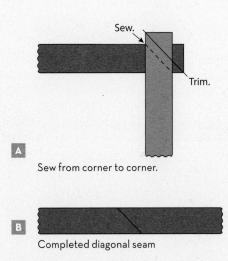

Sew.

Trim.

A Sew from corner to corner.

B Completed diagonal seam

Press the entire strip in half lengthwise with wrong sides together. With raw edges even, pin the binding to the front edge of the quilt a few inches away from a corner, and leave the first few inches of the binding unattached. Start sewing, using a ¼" seam allowance.

Stop ¼" away from the first corner (see Step 1) and backstitch 1 stitch. Lift the presser foot and needle. Rotate the quilt one-quarter turn. Fold the binding at a right angle so it extends straight above the quilt and the fold forms a 45° angle in the corner (see Step 2). Then bring the binding strip down even with the edge of the quilt (see Step 3). Begin sewing at the folded edge. Repeat in the same manner at all corners. **FIGURES C–E**

Continue stitching until you are back near the beginning of the binding strip. Cut both ends of the binding so that they overlap a scant 2¼".

Open both tails. Place 1 tail on top of the other tail at right angles, right sides together. Mark a diagonal line from corner to corner and stitch on the line. Check that you've done it correctly and that the binding fits the quilt; then trim the seam allowance to ¼". Press open. **FIGURE F**

Refold the binding and stitch this binding section in place on the quilt. Fold the binding over the raw edges to the quilt back and hand stitch.

Continuous Bias Binding

To make continuous bias binding from a square of fabric, follow the directions that can be found on the sidebar of my blog at amandamurphydesign.blogspot.com, or go to tinyurl.com/quiltmaking-basics and download the PDF "How to Finish Your Quilt."

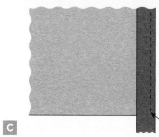

C

End stitching ¼" from corner.

Step 1. Stitch to ¼" from corner.

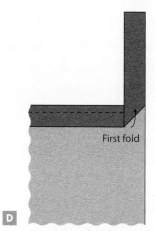

First fold

D

Step 2. First fold for miter

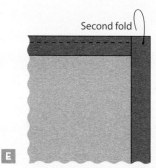

Second fold

E

Step 3. Second fold alignment

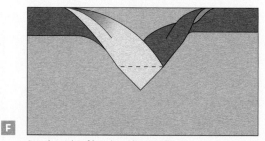

F

Stitch ends of binding diagonally.

About the Author

Always attracted to color, texture, and pattern, Amanda Murphy has been designing, drawing, and sewing since she was a child. After graduating with a bachelor of fine arts in design from Carnegie Mellon University, she worked as a graphic designer and art director

Photo by Elizabeth Sawyer-Menaker

in Alexandria, Virginia, and New York City. After moving to North Carolina with her family, Amanda discovered quilting, an art that marries her passion for design with her enthusiasm for handwork. As she gradually expanded her knowledge of quilting techniques and combined them with the ideas she had been sketching over the years, Amanda Murphy Design was born.

Amanda markets her own pattern line under the Amanda Murphy Design label and has designed several fabric collections for Blend Fabrics, a subsidiary of Anna Griffin Inc. She also designs embroidery motifs for OESD, distributed exclusively by Brewer and teaches online classes at Craftsy. com. Amanda's first book, *Modern Holiday*, came out in 2013.

Amanda hopes her books, fabrics, and quilt designs will inspire others to create their own works of art. Visit her websites and share designs you make from this book:

Website: amandamurphydesign.com

Blog: amandamurphydesign.blogspot.com

Flickr group: flickr.com/groups/color_essentials

Also by Amanda Murphy:

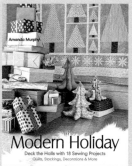

Supplies/Source List

Aurifil USA (*50-weight cotton piecing thread, 12- and 28-weight cotton thread for appliqué*)
aurifil.com

Bernina of America, Inc. (*Bernina 580e*)
berninausa.com • **WeAllSew.com**

Clover (*fusible bias tape maker, "quick" yo-yo maker*)
clover-usa.com

Creative Grids USA (*rulers*)
creativegridsusa.com

C&T Publishing (*fast2cut Dresden Plate Template*)
ctpub.com

Deborah's Quilting (*quilter*)
Deborah Norris
deborahs_quilting@hotmail.com
deborahsquilting.blogspot.com

Robert Kaufman Fabrics
robertkaufman.com • **swatchandstitch.com**

Simplicity (*Easy Dresden templates by Darlene Zimmerman*)
simplicity.com

Sulky of America (*Tear-Easy stabilizer*)
sulky.com

The Warm Company (*Warm & White batting, Warm & Natural batting, Lite Steam-A-Seam, and Lite Steam-A-Seam 2*)
warmcompany.com